P9-DEK-674

Goshen, IN

Preaching from Memory to Hope

Also by Thomas G. Long
from Westminster John Knox Press

Hebrews (Interpretation)
Matthew (Westminster Bible Companion)
Preaching as a Theological Task: World, Gospel, Scripture (coeditor)
Preaching In and Out of Season
The Senses of Preaching
Teaching Preaching as a Christian Practice (coeditor)
The Witness of Preaching

Preaching from Memory to Hope

THOMAS G. LONG

WESTMINSTER
JOHN KNOX PRESS
LOUISVILLE · KENTUCKY

© 2009 Thomas G. Long

All rights reserved. No part of this book may be reproduced or transmitted in any form or by any means, electronic or mechanical, including photocopying, recording, or by any information storage or retrieval system, without permission in writing from the publisher. For information, address Westminster John Knox Press, 100 Witherspoon Street, Louisville, Kentucky 40202-1396.

Scripture quotations from the New Revised Standard Version of the Bible are copyright © 1989 by the Division of Christian Education of the National Council of the Churches of Christ in the U.S.A. and are used by permission.

Excerpt from a sermon preached by Brooks Holifeld at Cannon Chapel, Emory University used by permission. Excerpt from funeral prayer from *Life Passages: Renewing Worship*, volume 4, copyright © Evangelical Lutheran Church in America, admin. Augsburg Fortress. Used by permission of Augsburg Fortress Publishers. Excerpt from "Gather Us In" by Marty Haugen, © 1983, GIA Publications, Inc., 7404 S. Mason Avenue, Chicago, IL 60638. Used by permission. Excerpt from Terry Eagleton, "Lunging, Flailing, Mispunching," *London Review of Books* 28/20 (Oct. 19, 2006) used by permission. Excerpt from *No Country for Old Men* by Cormac McCarthy, copyright © 2005 by M-71, Ltd. Used by permission of Alfred A. Knopf, a division of Random House, Inc. Excerpt from Charles Campbell, "Principalities, Powers, and Preaching: Learning from William Stringfellow," *Interpretation* 51/4 (Oct. 1997) used by permission. Excerpt from *True North*, by Jim Harrison, copyright © 2004 by Jim Harrison. Used by permission of Grove/Atlantic, Inc. Excerpt from Fleming Rutledge, *The Undoing of Death,* © 2005 Wm. B. Eerdmans Publishing Company, Grand Rapids, MI. Reprinted by permission of the publisher, all rights reserved.

Book design by Drew Stevens
Cover design by designpointinc.com

First edition
Published by Westminster John Knox Press
Louisville, Kentucky

This book is printed on acid-free paper that meets the American National Standards Institute Z39.48 standard. ∞

PRINTED IN THE UNITED STATES OF AMERICA

09 10 11 12 13 14 15 16 17 18—10 9 8 7 6 5 4 3 2 1

Library of Congress Cataloging-in-Publication Data

Long, Thomas G.
    Preaching from memory to hope / Thomas G. Long.—1st ed.
        p. cm.
    Includes index.
    ISBN 978-0-664-23422-5 (alk. paper)
    1. Preaching.   I. Title.
    BV4211.3.L65 2009
    251—dc22

                                                    2008039354

For Craig Dykstra

A true friendship is as wise as it is tender.
—Thoreau

Contents

Preface   ix

Introduction   xiii

1. A Likely Story: The Perils and Power
   of Narrative in Preaching   1

2. No News Is Bad News: God in the Present Tense   27

3. Nasty Suspicions, Conspiracy Theories,
   and the Return of Gnosticism   55

4. Meeting Marcus Borg Again for the First Time   79

5. Preaching in the Future-Perfect Tense: Eschatology
   and Proclamation   111

Notes   133

Index   145

Preface

On the wall of what my grandmother called the "sitting room" of her antebellum home in South Carolina was a constellation of family portraits—old pictures of my uncles and aunts, my cousins, grandparents and great-grandparents, a genealogy in photographs. In the very middle of the cluster, in the place of honor, was the portrait of someone I did not recognize. It was a sepia-toned, Civil War–era photograph of a striking young man dressed in the uniform of a Union army officer. Needless to say, this was very unusual—the portrait of a Yankee soldier in a place of honor on the wall of a proud South Carolina home. One day, when I was small child, I asked my grandmother, "Who is that man?"

She said, "I'll tell you when you're old enough to understand."

Years later, just before she died, she saw me in the sitting room one day, all by myself, gazing at the portrait. She came in, sat down beside me, and she finally told me the story. The man was a good man, she said, a minister, a chaplain in the Union Army. In May of 1862, after the smoke had cleared from the field of battle at Williamsburg, Virginia, this chaplain rode out onto the field on his horse to see if there were any wounded troops who had been left behind, and he came across a nineteen-year-old Confederate soldier, lying wounded and terrified in a ditch. The boy had taken a bullet that had practically severed his leg at the knee, and he was slowly bleeding to death. Feeling compassion, even for the enemy, the chaplain lifted the boy out of the ditch, put him on his horse, and took him to the Union medical tent, where a surgeon amputated his leg at the knee, bandaged him up, and stopped the bleeding, saving his life. When the boy was strong enough to travel, this chaplain got together enough money to see that he was sent home to his grateful and relieved parents in South Carolina.

This nineteen-year-old Confederate soldier grew up to be a minister himself, a teacher, a college president, and, what is most significant to me, my great-grandfather. The chaplain who rescued him and saved his life was the Rev. Joseph Twitchell, a ministerial graduate of Yale College and, after the war, a good friend of Mark Twain's and the minister of

Asylum Hill Congregational Church in Hartford, Connecticut, where among his parishioners were some of Lyman Beecher's children. Joseph Twitchell and my great-grandfather, William Moffatt Grier, bound together by this humane moment amid the ravages of war, remained correspondents and friends throughout the rest of their lives.

No one had to preach the parable of the Good Samaritan to my family. We had lived it.

I was able to tell the story of Joseph Twitchell and my great-grandfather when I delivered the Lyman Beecher Lectures at Yale Divinity School in the fall of 2006. I told it as a sign of the irony that pervades all of our lives, in particular the irony that the man who saved my great-grandfather was a graduate of Yale and pastor to the children of the one in whose memory the Beecher Lectures were established. But I told it also in gratitude. If it had not been for Joseph Twitchell, my great-grandfather would not have lived to see his twentieth birthday, and I would not, of course, have been born. If it had not been for Yale College and the other influences that shaped the man Joseph Twitchell, he would not have had the vision and compassion to roam a battlefield searching for the wounded and the dying. If he had not had the character to go out onto the abandoned field of conflict in Williamsburg, Virginia, and look in forlorn ditches for dying people, even for his enemies, I would not be around to be a great-grandson, a grandson, a son, a father, a husband, a pastor, a Christian theologian, and a lecturer at Yale Divinity School. The more we know of life, the more we know that all that we have is gift, all that we are is grace.

Chapters 1, 2, and 5 of this book are the 2006 Lyman Beecher lectures, expanded a bit to respond to queries and suggestions from those who first heard them and those who later read them in manuscript form. I am grateful to Yale Divinity School and to its superb dean, Professor Harold Attridge, for the invitation to deliver these lectures. The Lyman Beecher Lectures have been, during most of their 130-plus years of history, devoted to the excellence in the ministry preaching and stand as the Mount Everest of scholarship in the field of homiletics. I was humbled and awestruck to take my place in the long line of distinguished lecturers that has included Henry Ward Beecher, Phillips Brooks, P. T. Forsyth, Harry Emerson Fosdick, George Buttrick, Gardner Taylor, Barbara Brown Taylor, Fred Craddock, Walter Brueggemann, Samuel Proctor, David Bartlett, Walter Burghardt, Leander Keck, Peter Gomes, David Buttrick, Barbara Lundblad, Richard Lischer, and many others. I am grateful, also, to my good colleagues on the

Yale faculty, especially Nora Tisdale and Thomas Troeger, who provided personal support and warm hospitality during the lectures.

Chapters 3 and 4 include material on the rise of neo-gnosticism in the church, a theme that has intrigued me for several years. I am grateful to the congregations who suffered through and responded to early versions of this material: Westminster Presbyterian Church in Durham, North Carolina, and Fourth Presbyterian Church in Greenville, South Carolina, and to their dedicated pastors Haywood Holderness and Allen McSween. I am also indebted to the 2007 Washington Island Forum, sponsored by the *Christian Century* and the Wisconsin Council of Churches, and to the 2008 Florida Winter Pastors' School at Stetson University, hosted with grace by Bill O'Connor and Clyde Fant, where some of this material was presented, and to Duke Divinity School and to its able dean, L. Gregory Jones, who invited me to deliver the 2004 Jameson Jones lectures, in which I made my first attempts to address this topic.

Many good friends and colleagues have helped me think through the issues in these pages. I lack sufficient means to thank them, beyond being grateful. They are not responsible, naturally, for where I landed, but their air traffic control has made the flight possible. In particular I want to acknowledge Joy McDougall, Stephen Lösel, Stephen Kraftchick, Luke Timothy Johnson, Carl Holladay, Erskine Clarke, Elizabeth Bounds, Brooks Holifield, Gail O'Day, Rick Lischer, John Woods, Lance Pape, Matt Flemming, and the extraordinary students who formed my reading group in the theology of preaching last spring—Ben Anthony, Heather Bargeron, Parker Diggory, Joseph Gunby, Daniel Ogle, and Joshua Ralston. In addition, I want to express my appreciation to the McAfee School of Theology in Atlanta, to Dean Alan Culpepper, and to Dr. William L. Self for their superb hospitality during the 2007 Self Preaching Lectures, where some of the ideas in this book were presented. If the arguments in this volume have any value whatsoever, these are the people to be thanked.

Most of all, though, I want to express my deep gratitude to Craig Dykstra, who has been my dear friend for nearly four decades and to whom this book is dedicated. His role in my life and in my intellectual development is incalculable. I am blessed by his friendship in more ways than I can name.

Thomas G. Long
Candler School of Theology
Summer 2008

Introduction

About every fifty years American preaching has a nervous breakdown. What happens is that the trusted structures and strategies of the pulpit suddenly seem to lose their potency, and worried preachers, their confidence shaken, begin to scramble for the next, new thing. After decades of gliding blithely across the homiletical dance floor to the same familiar rhythms, it dawns on preachers that the music has changed, culturally and theologically, and they are out of step. The usual techniques, customary homiletical tactics, and prevailing assumptions about the task of preaching all seem questionable or even dubious. Something new is called for from the pulpit.

I am persuaded that we are now in such a time of upheaval. Part of the current shift has occurred because the prevailing image of the preacher as a "storyteller," which comes and goes in American preaching and has been with us this time in one form or another since the 1950s, has begun to leak around the gaskets. The cluster of homiletical styles and techniques that we have come to call "narrative preaching," once all the rage, now seems a bit tired. What used to bring hearers to the edge of their pews now often elicits a yawn or a bewildered look. (By the way, in the current homiletical glossary, "narrative preaching" is a term that embraces such features as a view of scripture as a collection of stories and other literary genres that together form a grand narrative; the use in sermons of contemporary "epiphanies," theologically freighted "real life" anecdotes; a notion that sermon structures should be built, not as logical arrangements of content, but much like the dynamic plots of short stories; and an emphasis upon metaphors, images, and other types of figurative language in preaching.)

But if preaching is undergoing an image makeover, it is also changing in response to the falling barometer of North American church life. If there is any truth to the jingle that Americans now desire to be "spiritual but not religious," then preaching is in a double bind. Many preachers wonder how to address in their sermons this new and restless spirituality and, at the same time, how not to look too churchy while doing it (after all, what is more "religious" than a sermon?). Small wonder, then, that many pastors have kicked into high experimental gear, infusing their sermons with new technologies (e.g., screens, video clips, 3-D holographic projection), new approaches (e.g., breakout discussion groups mid-sermon, bullet points and outlines printed in bulletins), new forms of delivery (e.g., wandering around the worship space like Odysseus), and even new wardrobes (e.g., sweaters, jeans, and Hawaiian shirts instead of robes, dark suits, and albs). Even the African American pulpit, which has historically managed to stay strong during the periodic pulpit meltdowns in the mainly white churches, is showing stress due to suburbanization, a fascination in some quarters with the so-called "prosperity gospel," and other forces.

One of the effects I am hoping for in this book is a certain calm in the midst of this storm. We have been through this kind of convulsion in preaching before. Time and again, preaching has appeared headed for the shoals, only to burst through the straights refreshed and reinvigorated. We have also been through many prior seasons of innovation. Multimedia sermons, first-person sermons, musical sermons, dialogue sermons, sermons preached from bar stools, silent sermons— these and many other experiments have been tried before. As Ecclesiastes says, "What has been is what will be, and what has been done is what will be done; there is nothing new under the sun" (Eccl. 1:9). We do not know exactly what a sermon will look and sound like fifty years from now. Perhaps the technological innovations will prove enduring, and almost every sermon in the mid-twenty-first century will include striking video and audio clips, dramatic skits serving as illustrations, and interactive features whereby hearers can instantly respond to the sermon electronically, influencing on the spot its flow and outcome. Or maybe such techniques, like 8-track tapes and pink bathrooms, will then seem like outdated fashion trends best left on the rubbish heap, and our homiletical grandchildren will wonder, "What were they thinking?" Who knows? What we do know, historically and theologically, is that preaching will still be around, as urgent and as demanding a ministry as ever. Preachers need to experiment with new forms and strategies, but not to panic. Like Jesus' description of the wise scribe, preaching will emerge from this experimental period bringing out of its homiletical treasure "what is new and what is old" (Matt. 13:52).

The main goal of this book, however, is not to turn calmness into complacency, but to take seriously what I consider to be the deeper regions of the current challenge to the pulpit. Rather than fidgeting with whether we should stay behind the pulpit or wander, use video clips or trust the spoken word alone, wear stoles or jeans, I want to lift up some of what I take to be the more substantive theological forces and issues facing preaching today. In chapter 1, I take a good hard look at the recent attacks on narrative preaching, and while I find much to attend to in these criticisms, I end up defending a chastened form of narrative preaching as essential to the proclamation of the gospel. In chapter 2, I describe the curious loss of the present tense in much contemporary preaching, namely, the reluctance of many preachers to name the presence and activity of God in our midst, and, building upon some insights from philosopher Paul Ricoeur, I suggest some ways to recover this emphasis. In chapters 3 and 4, I turn to the new spirituality both in the church and in the culture at large, and while others may welcome this burst of spiritual hunger, I find much of it to be an old nemesis, gnosticism, come back around to haunt us again. I suggest some ways for the pulpit to engage in a kind of interfaith dialogue with gnosticism. In the final chapter, I take up yet another neglected theme in preaching, eschatology, finding that many pastors, genuinely puzzled by the doctrine of the Parousia, embarrassed by the droolings of the *Left Behind* crowd, and outmaneuvered by the anti-eschatological bias of the new gnostics, have sadly chosen to roll up their windows and lock their doors while driving through the New Testament's eschatological neighborhoods.

Throughout this book, I try to call for a bold and joyful approach to preaching, preaching that stands out in the full force of the cultural gale, unafraid of the storm, preaching that can lovingly tell the story of God's people, courageously announce what God is doing among us, and confidently invite people to lean forward in hope toward the promises of God—preaching, in other words, that clearly and confidently proclaims God's past, present, and future to a spiritually disoriented age.

1

A Likely Story: The Perils and Power of Narrative in Preaching

People bleed stories, and I have become a blood bank of them.
— Anatole Broyard, *Intoxicated by My Illness*[1]

I was disappointed in the film. It has everything but a good story.
—Stanley Kubrick, on the release of *Sparticus*[2]

Not long ago, in my basic course in preaching, a piece of pedagogy blew up in my face. I was playing the recording of what I consider to be an absolutely superb sermon by one of America's most accomplished preachers. I have been using this same sermon in class for nearly a decade as an exquisite, state-of-the-art example of creative sermon form. One of the many virtues of this sermon is the way it uses stories, contemporary narratives, not as ornaments or mere illustrations but as theological fiber and muscle empowering the dance of the sermon's movement. In fact, this sermon ends with four brief, incandescent narratives, each cut like a gem, each performing its own unique task of advancing the sermon toward a stunning conclusion. It is a masterly example of the preaching craft, and it never fails to generate not only learning but admiration.

But not this time. To my surprise, the sermon left many of the students cold. They were bored and disoriented, particularly by the narratives. "Too many stories," said one of the students. "I felt overwhelmed by them." Another student, who I think may have missed the subtler shades of meaning, complained, "Why *did* he tell all those stories at the end? I was, like, 'Come on! I got the point after the *first* one.'"

At one level, of course, these were simply the responses of one group of students with their own preferences, their own reactions, their own peculiar group chemistry, and their negative responses generated a good conversation about style and listening. At another level, though, as I watched this young generation of students shrug their shoulders in bewilderment over what is, technically speaking, a homiletical tour de force, a beautifully crafted narrative sermon, I wondered if I was watching the canary die in the coal mine. For nearly fifty years, some form of narrative preaching has been the prevailing style in the American pulpit, but that approach to preaching is now beginning to take on water. It is being roundly challenged from many directions, including the underwhelming response of younger hearers like my students. We may well be in the midst of one of those seismic shifts in preaching style that occur periodically and that are expressions of deeper changes in culture, theology, and religious life, and my students that day may have been a generational barometer registering the drop in atmospheric pressure.

THE RISE OF NARRATIVE PREACHING

How is it that the last couple of generations of American preachers became fascinated by narrative? In the early 1950s, much of mainline Protestant preaching was highly didactic. Sermons were viewed as instruments of instruction about the great themes of the Christian faith. Sermons were often taken up with big principles and doctrinal propositions, and they were built to carry the freight. Almost all of the major preaching textbooks recommended that sermons be, like term papers and academic lectures, logical, orderly, balanced, and symmetrical, with clearly demarcated points and subpoints.

Things were tidy in the classroom, but all was not well in the actual pulpit. Although churches in the 1950s were mostly full of worshipers, preachers sensed a background hum of boredom. People were in worship and they were smiling, but they were not listening—not to the sermons anyway. And to be honest, much of the preaching of that era was not worth listening to. The imagination and intellectual energy had leaked out of much of popular Christianity, and there was a kind of listlessness in the pulpit. Read some typical sermons from the early 1950s, and many of them call to mind the criticism William McAdoo made of Warren Harding's stump speeches: "His speeches left the impression of an army of pompous phrases moving over the landscape in search of an idea. Sometimes these meandering words would actually capture a straggling thought and bear it triumphantly, a prisoner in their midst, until it died of servitude and overwork."

So, with the people bored and sermons not connecting, a distress signal went out from pulpits to homileticians, and starting in the midfifties, a revised approach to preaching was quietly born, both in theory and in practice. The first wave to break on the shore was H. Grady Davis's 1958 preaching textbook *Design for Preaching*, in which he argued that preachers should no longer think of sermons as didactic arguments with orderly points but as living organisms, moving, dynamic, growing; in other words, a preacher should imagine a sermon more like a short story than a legal brief. Here was a book that challenged the teachy style of most preaching, and it felt like a fresh breeze. *Design for Preaching* became the most popular preaching textbook in American seminaries for fifteen years.

In 1971, an even more remarkable skirmish with the prevailing pulpit style took place. Fred B. Craddock, then a professor of preaching and New Testament in Oklahoma, published the little book *As One without Authority*, arguably the most influential monograph on preaching in our time. Craddock called for preachers to abandon the top-down, deductive, "my thesis for this morning" approach to sermons in favor of suspenseful, inductive, narratives of discovery. Preachers were to stop telling people what the sermon was about in the introduction and were instead to lure people along on a journey of exploration and surprise with real-life stories and questions to the place where they could exclaim, "Aha! I get it!" at the end of the sermon.

In his Lyman Beecher Lectures, delivered at Yale in 1978, Craddock extended his emphasis on story preaching. He built his lectures around a line from Søren Kierkegaard: "There is no lack of information in a Christian land; something else is lacking, and this is something which the one [person] cannot directly communicate to the other."[3] Craddock took Kierkegaard's observation about Denmark in the nineteenth century to be also an apt description of the American Protestant landscape in the 1970s. There is no lack of information; we have been taught and Sunday-schooled to the point of suffocation. What is lacking is something else: personal, existential engagement with the gospel. And that cannot be communicated directly—point one, point two, point three—but only indirectly through induction, story, and metaphor.

In 1980, another teacher of preaching, Eugene Lowry, published the widely used and enormously influential preaching textbook *The Homiletical Plot*, which claimed that what really gets the juices going for hearers is not learning about ideas but resolving ambiguity, and thus, good sermons should be built on the chassis of a narrative plot that moves sequentially from stirring up ambiguity to resolving it, from conflict to climax to denouement.

The authors of one state-of-the-art textbook from this period, aptly called *Preaching the Story,* engaged in a bit of rhetorical flourish by declaring that they were searching around for the perfect master image to gather up the whole of the preaching task in a single stitch. "We are trying," they said,

> to find that formative image that could both articulate what preaching is and free people to do it. Is there an image adequate to shape the form, content, and style of preaching? If we had to say, in a word or two, or in a picture, what preaching is and how it is done well, what would that phrase or picture be? . . . Let us consider the storyteller. . . . If we were pressed to say what Christian faith and life are, we could hardly do better than *hearing, telling, and living a story.* And if asked for a short definition of preaching, could we do better than *shared story?*[4]

The world of preaching was tilting on its axis, and a whole cottage industry of books on the new narrative style—story preaching, metaphors, images, and plots—mushroomed. Dialogue sermons, short-story sermons, first-person sermons, image-rich sermons, autobiographically confessional sermons, and more abounded. The varieties were endless, but all of them riffs on the notion that good preaching was somehow story shaped, story saturated, story driven.

American preaching in this period was actually fighting on two fronts. There was the miasma of boredom rising from the pews but there was also, especially in the late 1960s and early 1970s, a nagging suspicion about the usefulness of the whole preaching enterprise building among clergy themselves. In the social upheavals of the times, nothing seemed more presumptuous, antiquated, irrelevant, and hopelessly authoritarian than the act of preaching. Hang out a shingle as a pastoral therapist, or get out in the streets as an agent of social change, but don't waste your time fogging up the sanctuary by preaching. Many seminaries during this period eliminated required courses in preaching. So the idea of a kinder, gentler, more engaging story style of preaching brought an infusion of energy, excitement, and purpose to a dispirited pulpit, and the narrative approach was seized like a life preserver.

It should be said, I suppose, that when it comes to the actual practitioners, to the parish preachers, that the surge in narrative preaching came more through imitation than through application. The homiletical books explained narrative preaching, justified it, and provided theoretical backfill, but preaching, as Augustine taught us, is often learned through imitation first and reflection second. What got narrative preaching going full steam were the sermons of preachers like Edmund Steimle, who stunned listeners of *The Protestant Hour* radio program with his unconventional narrative, conversational sermons; Frederick Buechner, whose books of imaginative narrative sermons were on the shelves of countless preachers; and Fred Craddock, James Forbes, and later Barbara Brown Taylor, who traveled from congregation to college to conference, charming listeners with their gifts for narrative and imaginative preaching. These preachers, with their angular biblical exegesis, wry humor, gripping images, and moving stories hit the American pulpit like the Beatles hit the charts.

The American church had grown weary of the grandiloquent pulpit princes with their big voices and their abstract principles and their dramatic gestures and their pedantic sermons and their overblown moral lessons. The times were ripe for change, and along come these preachers with their winsome styles and different voices and ability to see the biblical characters as people with ordinary lives who lived in the next neighborhood. These preachers sounded less like pulpit royalty and more like wise friends rocking on a country porch. Suddenly pulpits everywhere were filled with imitators (and they still are), preachers who experimented and learned to begin their sermons not with "Dear Christian friends, I wish to tell you three things this morning about the power of prayer," but "When I was a child, there was in our little town an old man with a wrinkled face who worked in Gibson's Hardware . . ."

Augustine said, in the very first homiletical textbook in the history of the church, *De doctrina christiana*, book IV, that the purpose of a sermon is "to teach, to delight, and to persuade." He borrowed that line from Cicero, but Augustine lassoed it and corralled it into a Christian thought. The first responsibility of a preacher, he said, is to teach the content of the gospel, but the content needs to be taught not pedantically but delightfully, taught in such a way that it excites the imagination and inflames the heart. If the gospel is taught delightfully, then it will be persuasive, by which Augustine meant that it will open up ways of being and living ethically in the world. When the substance of the gospel is taught with imagination, then the Christian life becomes an imaginable possibility. When Augustine preached, what he wanted to hear at the door of the church was not, "Thank you for your little talk," but "I learned something this morning, I was moved by what you said, and I intend to do something about it." To teach, to delight, and to persuade.

Augustine was describing the goals of individual sermons—to teach, delight, and persuade—but he also inadvertently described seasons in the history of preaching. There are cultural moments that require the inflection to slant this way or that. There are times when the pulpit needs to become a lectern, and the emphasis falls on teaching the people. And there are times of urgent crisis, when the pulpit raises even higher the prophet's torch and the voice of preaching becomes commandingly ethical. But what has happened since the mid-1950s is that American preaching has been basking in a season of delight. In the middle of the twentieth century, American Christianity was bored and disengaged. People had been taught well but not enchanted. People had heard the instruction and the moral injunctions of the faith. What they were missing was delight.

This generation of American preachers is not the first to have been fascinated with stories and narration. Like Halley's comet, narrative preaching comes around periodically as the method of choice, usually when the didactic vessels have become too small to contain gushing new forms of religious experience. Historian David Reynolds makes the case that this is actually the third time around for narrative preaching to be in vogue in the American pulpit.[5] The first narrative surge peaked in the early nineteenth century when Methodist evangelists and southern black preachers, using folklore styles, built narrative castles on the land vacated by the collapse of Puritan homiletics, with their sermons amply stocked with dozens of logical points and subpoints.[6] Eventually this more narrative style made its way to New England, and even Boston Unitarians began experimenting with it, although in more polished and literary fashion.[7]

The second round of narrative preaching in America came later in the nineteenth century, led by such preachers as T. DeWitt Talmage, Phillips Brooks, Dwight L. Moody, and Henry Ward Beecher. Beecher practically invented the modern sermon anecdote as he experimented with rhetorical style in his sermons to his Brooklyn congregation. These preachers were, to a greater or lesser degree, breaking loose from scholastic theologies and surfing on a cresting wave of humanist thought, from Emerson to Bushnell, which saw human life itself as the great religious text. To tell stories about the depths of human life was to tell sacred narratives.

In his 1838 address to the Harvard divinity students, Emerson famously commented on preaching, remarks that signaled changes to come. He said that he had once heard a preacher who made him want never to go to church again. While the man was preaching, the congregation could see through the church windows a snow storm blowing outside, and the comparison between the swirling storm and the lifeless preacher was painful. "The snow storm," said Emerson,

> was real; the preacher merely spectral; and the eye felt the sad contrast in looking at him, and then out of the window behind him, into the beautiful meteor of the snow. He had lived in vain. He had not one word intimating that he had laughed or wept, was married or in love, had been commended, or cheated, or chagrined. If he had ever lived and acted, we were none the wiser for it. The capital secret of his profession, namely, to convert life into truth, he had not learned. Not one fact in all his experience, had he yet imported into his doctrine. This man had ploughed, and planted, and talked, and bought, and sold; he had read books; he had eaten and drunken; his head aches; his heart throbs; he smiles and suffers; yet was there not a surmise, a hint, in all the discourse, that he had ever lived at all. . . . The true preacher can be known by this, that he deals out to the people his life—life passed through the fire of thought.[8]

For the last generation of preachers, then, what had come around before has come around again, and the pulpit has indeed been dealing out Emerson's wish for "life passed through the fire of thought" and doing so by spinning stories.

NARRATIVE PREACHING FACES THE CRITICS

Every wave of narrative preaching generates critics. John Wesley warned his storytelling colleagues not to be feeding people narrative "sweetmeats" and "cordials." Commenting on the emotionalism of the late nineteenth century and the narrative style that carried it, historian Henry Steele Commager remarked that "during the nineteenth century religion prospered in America while theology went slowly bankrupt."[9]

And as for the narrative revival in our time, from the very beginning there were doubters. I will never forget an incident that occurred at a meeting of the Academy of Homiletics in the mid-1970s, a time when highly experimental forms of narrative preaching were becoming all the rage. I arrived at the meeting several hours late, after the group had already been treated to several edgy papers raving about story preaching. As I made my way into the meeting room, bursting out of the room, his eyes wild, was Ron Sleeth, a well-respected teacher of preaching who had a long and distinguished academic career. When he saw me heading in, he grabbed my shoulders and said, "Don't go in there, Tom. The crazies have taken over the Academy!" Story preaching, he harrumphed later in an essay, is nothing but "private parables in the name of self-expression."[10]

At the height of interest in story preaching, Richard Lischer of Duke Divinity School warned that preaching is like a dinghy tied to a ship's stern that takes on all the flotsam of culture that washes from the ship's wake. Lischer predicted that we would one day grow tired of narrative. "How long after theology has tired of story and our culture has grown bored with finding itself will preaching be burdened by the weight of this cargo that washed aboard one stormy night in the seventies?"[11]

These critics, however, were lonely voices. But now, a chorus of critics has begun to sing, and story preaching has come under fire from the theological right, the theological middle, and the theological left. From the right, evangelicals were slow to warm to story preaching and quick to cool to it. Even though narrative preaching made inroads into the evangelical world, they were always nervous that story preaching was too soft, too doctrinally unclear, too ethically ambiguous, and too shy about evangelism. Recently, James W. Thompson at Abilene Christian University has done a sophisticated critique of narrative homiletics from an evangelical perspective. Narrative homiletics, he charges, wrongly assumes a Christian culture already in place, focuses on the form of the sermon to the neglect of the larger theological aims of the sermon, limits the capacities of hearers to think rationally and reflectively about the faith, is reluctant to press demands for ethical change, and is weak at building and sustaining communities of faith.[12]

Lying under these and other worries about narrative preaching from the theological right may lurk an anxiety about the inherent ambiguity of narrative. In a time when Christians are confused about their identity and need crisp clarity and definition, narrative seems to have a dangerous tendency to muddy the waters all the more. Susan Wise Bauer, who has traced the tug of war among American conservatives and evangelicals over the last two centuries concerning the use of "narrative hymns" (hymns that focus on the story of human religious experience) versus "systematic hymns" (those that give priority to doctrine, logically presented), observed,

> Conservative wariness of narratives may have to do with a desire to police identities. The flexibility and ambiguity of narrative allow for experiences of faith different than our own. Narrative theologian

Johann Baptist Metz writes that marginal groups always employ 'not argument and reasoning, but narrative'; they tell stories about their experience because this 'refusal to speak the language of ritual and theology' is the only way to express a different grasp of reality than those who rule a culture or situation. Those who view themselves at the "center" are much more likely to employ doctrinal, logical language.[13]

Critics in the middle have also begun to have qualms about narrative preaching, which may work well in a church that is bored, but perhaps not so well in a theologically amnesiac culture. If a congregation knows the content of the Christian faith, but lacks passionate engagement with it, then bring on the stories. But what if the content is missing? Kierkegaard in the nineteenth century and Craddock in the 1970s may have claimed that "there is no lack of information in a Christian land," but now there *is* a lack of information, and it *isn't* a Christian land. Story sermons depend largely upon evocation; they blow narrative breath on the coals of latent knowledge and conviction, and they function best among people who have been well taught but who lack a deep sense of delight about what they have been taught. But in a culture in which those memories, convictions, and churchly patterns are not there to evoke and revivify, narrative preaching can easily end up being like a massage at a spa, a pleasurable aesthetic experience without content or goal.

Another charge from the middle against story preaching comes from Charles L. Campbell. In his powerfully argued book *Preaching Jesus*, he claims that a good bit of what passes for narrative preaching has been fastened to the wrong narratives, that it consists of superficial anecdotes of human experience or alleged plot structures in the imagination, rather than the gospel narratives. Drawing upon the work of Hans Frei, Campbell claims that "what is important for Christian preaching is not 'stories' in general or even 'homiletical plots,' but rather a specific story that renders the identity of a particular person. . . . [P]reaching in which Jesus is not the subject of his own predicates—comes in for critique."[14]

More recently, it has been critics from the left who have expressed profound displeasure with the narrative preaching. In fact, their attacks are the most severe of all, since they allege that practitioners of the "new" homiletics are not merely rhetorically mistaken, theologically weak, and trendy, but they have committed the far more serious offenses of potential oppression and abuse of power.

How do narrative preachers commit these crimes? By doing what narrative preachers do best, speaking from and to the common life experiences of the hearers. One of the sharpest critics on the left, John McClure of Vanderbilt Divinity School, draws on the work of Levinas to argue that the kind of stories that narrative preachers tend to tell carry the implied message, "Here is an everyday experience that we all have had or could have had, and if you really knew how to look at this experience, you would recognize it as a sacred experience." But in this seemingly gentle gesture of telling such stories, these preachers, McClure seems to say, have exercised their privileged positions of power to grind down all human differences, have lifted their own views of experience to the level of the universal and commanded the hearers to fit their lives into this frame. Moreover, they have insisted that people see God at work in every little nook and cranny of life and in just the way the preachers do, all the while hiding behind a false front of seemingly neutral and objective but really power-laden language. McClure aims right for the jugular of the cozy gospel storytellers (among others) when he says,

> God should not become too accessible, too easily located, too easily associated with symbols elevated to kerygmatic status within the tradition . . . or associated with symbols that may derive their meanings from subtle juxtapositions with what are largely hegemonic forms of human experience.[15]

In addition to these theological critiques from all directions, narrative has recently come in for a lashing by the British philosopher Galen Strawson. In his essay "Against Narrativity,"[16] Strawson identifies two theses that he states have widespread acceptance in academic fields as diverse as philosophy, psychology, literary studies, and theology. The first of these is the "psychological Narrativity thesis," namely, "that human beings typically see or live or experience their lives as a narrative or story of some sort, or at least as a collection of stories."[17] The second Strawson calls the "ethical Narrativity thesis," namely, "that experiencing or conceiving one's life as a narrative is a good thing; a richly Narrative outlook is essential to a well-lived life, to true or full personhood."[18] The two theses, Strawson states, are not necessarily logically linked. One may hold to the first, for example, but not to the second, believing that people do indeed see their lives as a narrative but that this is not a good thing. Or they may hold to the second (people *should* live out a narrative) but not to the first (but they typically do not), and so on.

Let me step to the side here to observe that Christians, it seems to me, have something at stake in both of these narrative theses. The scriptures begin not with a set of principles or proverbs but with the voice of a narrator, a storyteller: "In the beginning when God created the heavens and the earth, the earth was a formless void and darkness covered the face of the deep" (Gen. 1:1–2), and they end with a worshipful cry for the story of God to move to its next, dramatic chapter: "Amen. Come, Lord Jesus!" (Rev. 22:20). The Bible contains diverse literary forms and genres, but they are all enclosed in a grand narrative parenthesis. To the eye of faith, to be human is to be a creature, and to be a creature is to be enmeshed in the story of creation. A major theme in the theology of baptism, to name another place of narrative investment, is that through baptism Christians are gathered up into the identity of Jesus Christ, which means at least in part that we now see our lives in the shape and pattern of the story of Jesus. Jesus is, as Hebrews puts it, the "pioneer and perfecter of our faith" (Heb. 12:2). He has blazed the trail ahead of us, and his story is now our story. This narrative identity conveyed in baptism is both gift and disclosure. We are given a story about ourselves we could not have crafted on our own, but this story also discloses the truth about us that may have been hidden from our eyes, namely, that we have been created in the image of God and have always been a part of God's story. So, regarding Strawson's two narrative theses, Christians certainly hold to the second one—living out one's life as a Christ-shaped story is a good thing—but have a more nuanced view of the first one. Do people see themselves as living out a story? Some do and some don't, but Christians are bold to claim that people are living out some kind of narrative, even when they do not grasp this existentially. To be human is to live a story; to be an ethical human is to be gathered up into a good story.

Strawson, however, finds views like those expressed in the previous paragraph to be quite "regrettable" and even obstructionist. Figuratively pounding on the table, he says:

> It is just not true that there is only one good way for human beings to experience their being in time. There are deeply non-Narrative people and there are good ways to live that are deeply non-Narrative. I think [views that hold to the ethical Narrativity thesis] hinder human self-understanding, close down important avenues of thought, impoverish our grasp of ethical possibilities, needlessly and wrongly distress those who do not fit their model, and are potentially destructive in psychotherapeutic contexts.[19]

Strawson then proceeds to divide humanity into Diachronics, those who figure themselves "as something that was there in the (further) past and will be there in the (further) future," that is, people who tend to take a narrative outlook on life, and Episodics, those who don't. Diachronics and Episodics are prone to misunderstand each other, Strawson says. Diachronics look at Episodics, shake their heads, and feel "there is something chilling, empty and deficient about the Episodic life." Episodics, for their part, may frown on Diachronics, seeing their lives as "somehow macerated or clogged . . . or excessively self-concerned, inauthentically second-order."[20]

Strawson sees himself as a "relatively Episodic" person, and he takes up the Episodic cause, not as a way of dismissing Diachronics ("some of my closest friends" are Diachronics, he quips), but to insist that the "strongly Episodic life is one normal, non-pathological form of life for human beings and indeed one good form of life for human beings."[21]

Strawson's argument takes many fascinating twists and turns, but following it to the end is beyond our purpose here. What is within our purpose is to consider how Strawson describes himself and other Episodics. Strawson says that he is aware, naturally, that he has a past, and he can remember many of his past experiences. He remembers, for example, that he once fell out of a boat. "And yet," he says, "I have absolutely no sense of my life as a narrative with form. Absolutely none. Nor do I have any great or special interest in my past. Nor do I have a great deal of concern for my future."[22] As an Episodic, Strawson lives in a series of present tense moments. The past is alive, for him, only in the sense that it has shaped his present, much as a concert pianist's practice last Thursday afternoon is present in the movement of the fingers in the performance on Saturday night.[23] Strawson has no narrative, wants no narrative, and needs no narrative.

So narrative preaching is catching it these days from the philosophers, from the theological right, middle, and left, and at multiple levels. The theological right zings most sharply at the level of churchly practice: the telling of stories may ease minds and entertain the choir, but it doesn't build churches and extend the body of Christ. The middle has an educational complaint: the telling of stories may educe theological knowledge when it is already in place, but it doesn't supply it when it is not. For the theological left, the challenge is ethical. Storytelling enforces through coercion a monochromatic world upon the multihued experiences of others. The philosophers raise structural and ethical questions about the narrative epistemology and the assumptions about ethics and anthropology that undergird the whole storytelling enterprise.

Each of the attacks on narrative deserves a more lengthy response than I can give. Briefly, though, I think each of them constitutes a serious, but not fatal, challenge to narrative preaching. Those critics from the theological right aptly remind us that humanity does not live by narrative alone, but by every word that comes from the mouth of God, and thus the pulpit needs to sound forth with more than one voice. Their critique of narrative preaching is nonetheless tempered when we recognize that, in the linguistic repertoire of the gospel, narrative is not just one arrow in the quiver but is, in a sense, the quiver that holds all of the other arrows. Whenever Paul is carving out doctrine or exhorting his readers ethically or giving advice about worship, all of these forms of address assume narratives—the story of Israel, the story of Jesus, the mythic narrative of redemption—on which they rest and from which they spring. Always to tell stories means failure at the doctrinal, ethical, and practical tasks. Always to cut to the chase by preaching dogmatic instruction, exhortations, and church-building wisdom is to tear the gospel from its roots.

The critics from the middle land their best blows not on the glass jaw of narrative, but on the wrongful use of narrative. Simply to tell sermon stories about hikes in the wilderness or the vacation when the preacher sat on the beach and watched the sun sink impressively into the Pacific, confident that these narratives will massage deep theological memories in the hearts of the hearers of the glory of God in creation, is surely naive in a church culture where those memories are not firmly in place. But narrative is a flexible genre, and properly employed it can move beyond simply evocation to education and formation.

The critics from the left score some nice points about the potentially coercive effect of narrative, but they exaggerate the problem. People have the ability to move into narratives, even narratives of terror and stories of people quite unlike themselves, and then to return to their real lives informed and moved, perhaps, but not essentially damaged by the experience. One of the astonishing virtues of the human imagination is our ability to enter into stories of aliens from Mars, slave ships crossing the Atlantic in the eighteenth century, the czars of Russia, NASCAR drivers in Alabama, or whaling communities in Massachusetts and to lose ourselves in the story, but never to forget that it is a story. The best warning from the left, it seems to me, is regarding the cumulative effect of sermon narratives. One story is just one story; twenty stories create a world, and preachers would do well to question the ethical implications of one's repertoire of sermon stories. In this narrative world, who holds power and who does not? What is God like, and what is the human condition?

As for Strawson's antinarrative argument, he and I will, I suppose, simply have to agree to disagree about the validity of the Narrativity theses. But Strawson does us a service when he identifies a perhaps overlooked constituency among our congregations: the Episodics who are surely out there listening to our sermons. Now it is probably true that most of us have, at one and the same time, traits of both Diachronics and Episodics. Ask a card-carrying Diachronic to tell you about herself, and she will inevitably get around to telling the story of her life. But if that story is honestly told, it will recount many hours and days when the fragments, broken pieces, and disconnected episodes of her life seemed much more prominent than the plot line. To believe that you are living out a story does not mean that you never lose your place. Likewise, I suspect that even convinced Episodics now and then catch a glimpse of some larger narrative into which, willingly or unwillingly, they have been drawn and which arranges, however loosely, the discrete episodes of their lives.

We may, therefore, be blends of Episodic and Diachronic tendencies, but Strawson's challenge for preaching is that he highlights that portion of hearers (and probably a growing portion) that primarily experience life episodically. Many approaches to narrative preaching—Lowry's plotted sermons and Craddock's inductive sermons particularly come to mind—require that listeners be Diachronics, that they track the narrative structure from the opening sentence all the way through to the denouement. But what if (and this is not Strawson's point, I know, but he stirs it up) we are preaching to many Episodics who either cannot track the narrative plot or have no interest in doing so? They will probably seize upon some meaningful moment in the sermon, turn it into a "park bench" for reflection, and let the rest of it go.

Some megachurch preachers have seemingly noticed, or perhaps intuited, an increased presence of episodic listeners and have, in response, begun fashioning "antinarrative" sermons (my term, not theirs), sermons that are built as a series of stand-alone "bullet points." (We have perhaps returned in a digital age to the old "three-points-and-a-poem" style, except it's now "eight bullet points and a video clip." As one critic quipped, "When all you have are bullet-points, your ammunition is pretty quickly spent."[24]) Hearers are invited to browse these sermons as they would a Web page, skipping here and there as interest would allow. Such preaching is immediately engaging to many people, but it tends to reinforce the fragmented, nonnarrated character of contemporary life, and it works, at a deep level, against the gospel. Narrative preachers, however, can learn something important from this approach. We may now be in a communicational moment when narrative preaching as it has often been practiced is not viable. If we tell stories in sermons—biblical and otherwise—we will need also to step away from those stories and think them through in nonnarrative ways, drawing out explicitly the ideas and ethical implications of the stories. In short, preachers today may need to model in the sermon itself the internal processing of narratives that a previous generation of preachers could entrust fully to the hearers.

For example, in a splendid sermon on the passion story in the Gospel of Mark, Episcopal priest Fleming Rutledge, after naming the crucifixion of Jesus as the theme of the biblical passage and of the sermon, tells a personal story:

> I had a dear friend, whom I will call Sarah. When she was in her thirties, she developed rheumatoid arthritis and aplastic anemia and a host of other ills. For thirty years she suffered more physical pain and more crippling disabilities than almost anyone else I have ever known. We prayed for her constantly, to no apparent avail. Her husband said, "Every time we pray, she gets worse." I have never ceased to think about this friend, Sarah, whom I loved. If the Christian faith has nothing to say to her, it has nothing to say to anyone.[25]

Even though this story is brief, it has an emotional punch. The plaintive cry of the husband is especially moving: "Every time we pray, she gets worse." The biblical story of Jesus' passion is the master narrative for this sermon, but this story may be so familiar, or conversely so distantly unfamiliar, to the hearers that it has lost its power to generate emotion. But this is not so with the Sarah story. When the preacher places this contemporary pastoral experience next to the biblical passion story, energy flows between them. The preacher has connected the battery of the Sarah story to the engine of the biblical passion story. To put this into Augustine's terms, the story of Sarah is told to provide "delight," not in the superficial sense of pleasure, but in the deeper sense of moving the emotions.

Now one could imagine an approach to narrative preaching that would have encouraged the preacher to leave it pretty much at that, to allow these two narratives—the story of Jesus' suffering and the story of Sarah's suffering—to stand side by side without drawing the tether between them very tightly. Each story, the biblical and the contemporary, would supply energy for the other. The story of Jesus' passion

would provide a theological frame for the story of Sarah's pain; recipro-
cally, the emotional effect of Sarah's plight would siphon into the hearing of the biblical narrative. The preacher could trust the narrative form
to accomplish this transfer and need not—in fact should not—drain
away the power of these narratives by doing much explaining of the
connection between them. The goal would be for the listeners, not the
preacher, to "close the loop," for the listeners to rise to the preacher's
challenge at the end of the Sarah story by creatively filling in the blanks
and by naming for themselves what the passion story of Jesus has to say
to Sarah's situation.

Rutledge, though, quite rightly recognizes that in today's preaching
environment much more is needed; narrative cannot do all of the work
(and this may well have been what went wrong with the classroom sermon described at the outset of this chapter). Narrative is a powerful
tool, but if the teaching and ethical tasks of Christian preaching are to
be done, other strategies will also be needed. Very soon, then, after
telling the story of Sarah, Rutledge steps out of the storytelling posture
to assume two other voices: the voice of the teacher and voice of the
ethical guide. First, she teaches by responding theologically to her own
challenge about what the Christian faith can say to experiences of
human suffering like Sarah's:

> Jesus' Cry of Dereliction on the Cross is not just the heartbreaking
> lament of an abandoned man. It is that, but it is not only that. What
> we see and hear in Jesus' death is not just his identification with the
> wretched of the earth. It is that, but not only that. What we see and
> hear in Jesus' death is the decisive intervention of God to deliver his
> children from the unspeakable fate of ultimate abandonment. It is
> the strangest imaginable teaching on this most strange of all days.
> The testimony of the four evangelists, the testimony of the Christian
> church, is that in this event, in this godforsaken death, the cosmic
> scale has been conclusively tipped in the opposite direction, so that
> sin and evil and death are not the last word and never will be again.[26]

She says more in this vein, but notice already how she is guiding the
hearers in how to use the stories she has told. She allows the obvious
emotional connections to be made between Sarah' story and the passion
story, but she will not let the hearers be content to stay at this level. The
crucial issue at hand is not merely that Jesus suffered like Sarah, or even
that Jesus feels Sarah's pain because he identifies with her as a sufferer
(i.e., "It is that, but it is not only that"). She moves beyond the simple

emotional overlap and teaches an explicitly theological and christological idea—namely, that in Jesus' suffering God was at work defeating evil and depriving it of the last word about Sarah or anyone else—a claim that the hearers may well have been unable to supply for themselves.

But what should the hearers do with this theological claim? Again, some narrative approaches to preaching would have cautioned the preacher not to be overly concerned about this basically ethical question. What to do with the claims of the sermon is the business of the hearer, not the preacher. Since the hearers are presumably already aware that they are living out the Christian narrative, they can absorb the energy and experience of this sermon into the pattern of their lives and make ethical sense of it for themselves. But when many hearers have, in fact, lost their grip on the gospel story and are struggling to form a coherent Christian life, making ethical sense of things for themselves may well be precisely what they cannot do, or are reluctant to do. So, Rutledge, who has been both storyteller and teacher, now becomes a moral guide, choosing in this case to speak in confessional language:

> As long as there are people crying "God save me" in their own blood, how can we speak of deliverance in Jesus Christ? Do we just have to fall back on blind faith? Do we just say that God will make everything right one day?
>
> I am convinced that we can say more than that. Even as I am confronted with the intolerable fact of these words in blood, I am reminded also of the reasons I believe in the reality and the power of Jesus Christ even now in this "present evil age" (Gal. 1:4), even while it is hidden in the weakness of the servants of God.
>
> I believe that the Cross of Christ inaugurated the New World Order of God. It brought something into the world that was not there before. I believe in it because of those who follow that Way. [And now Rutledge moves back into storytelling voice] I think for instance of Susan Leckrone, a member of our New York City congregation, who at this moment is in Monrovia, Liberia ("the city of dreadful sights"), bathing out of a bucket because there is no running water, using her skills as a nurse to bring the love of Jesus to the victims of an atrocious civil war. She writes back and tells us that the Christians there are still praising the Lord.[27]

Rutledge's sermon, with its interplay of the narrative, the didactic, and the ethical, models a version of the kind of preaching that may well be emerging in responsible pulpits. She is a storyteller, and the sermon delights. But she not only delights; she teaches and persuades as well. She moves in and out of narrative voice, using the narratives explicitly to instruct and to explore the ethical implications of the gospel story. In this sense, the sermon is shaped much like the communicational pattern of the Gospel of Matthew (which is itself formed much like an early synagogue sermon), namely, as a rhythmic movement between haggadah (i.e., "the story") and halakah (i.e., "the way," that is, teaching and ethics).

NARRATIVE PREACHING REVISED

While I am not fully convinced by any of the arguments against narrative preaching, I am chastened by all of them, and persuaded by them of two truths: First, we no longer live in a sleeping Christendom waiting only to be aroused and delighted by evocative stories. The culture has shifted, and we need to take up with purpose Augustine's two other terms: teaching and ethical speech. Preaching today is going to need to learn to speak in multiple voices, some of them more direct, commanding, and urgent than narrative. The power in Christian preaching comes not only from narration but also from declaration ("Christ has been raised from the dead!"), explanation ("If for this life only we have hoped in Christ, we are of all people most to be pitied"), invitation ("Be steadfast, immovable, always excelling in the work of the Lord"), confession ("By the grace of God, I am what I am"), and even accusation ("O death, where is your victory?"). Every rhetorical instrument of human truth telling needs to be pressed into the service of proclaiming the gospel, and must become obedient to that gospel.

But second, in the light of the vigorous critique of the sloppier kinds of narrative preaching, preachers do not need to abandon storytelling but to get theologically smarter and more ethically discerning in its practice. What are we doing when we responsibly tell contemporary stories in sermons? We can point to four valuable and enduring uses of narratives in sermons:

1. *Narrative as Dress Rehearsal.* Aptly told stories do not simply make sermons interesting, touching, or emotionally powerful. Narrative is not merely a rhetorical device to titillate bored listeners. What we are doing, first of all, is dress rehearsing in the pulpit a competence expected of every Christian, the capacity to make theological sense out of the events and experiences of our lives. We want every Christian to struggle with the theological realities embedded in our national exercise of power and pride and deception in Iraq, embedded in the ambiguities of an ethical

decision at work, embedded in the seeming mundaneness of a checkout line at Wal-Mart on a Thursday afternoon and to see these as narrative arenas of faith and discernment. H. Richard Niebuhr put it well:

> [B]ecause the Christian community remembers the revelatory moment in its own history, it is required to regard all events . . . as workings of the God who reveals [the divine self], and so to trace . . . the ways of God in [human lives]. It is necessary for the Christian community, living in faith, to look upon all the events of time and to try to find in them the workings of one mind and will.[28]

Some years ago a funeral was held for Grace Thomas in the First Baptist Church of Decatur, Georgia. Not many people remember Grace Thomas today; indeed I had almost forgotten about her myself until I chanced across her obituary in an old newspaper and had my memory of her stirred.

Grace was the daughter of a Birmingham, Alabama, streetcar conductor and his wife. When she married in the late 1930s, she moved to Atlanta and took a clerking job in one of the state government offices. Through her work, she developed an interest in law and politics, and she enrolled in a local law school that offered night classes.

After years of part-time study, she finally completed law school, and her family wondered what she would do with her law degree. They were shocked when Grace announced that she had decided to enter the 1954 election race for governor of Georgia. There were nine candidates for governor that year, eight men and Grace, but there was really only one issue. In the famous *Brown v. the Board of Education* case earlier that year, the Supreme Court had declared racially "separate but equal" schools unconstitutional and thus paved the way for integration of the public schools. Eight of the gubernatorial candidates spoke out angrily against the court's decision. Only Grace said that she thought the decision was fair and just and ought to be welcomed by the citizenry. Her campaign slogan was "Say Grace at the Polls." Not many did; she ran dead last, and her family was relieved that she had gotten this out of her system.

But she had not. Eight years later, in 1962, she ran for governor again. By then, the civil rights movement was gaining momentum, and her message of racial harmony was hotly controversial. She received death threats, and her family traveled with her as she campaigned, in order to provide protection and moral support. She finished last again on election day, but her campaign was a testimony to goodwill and racial tolerance.

One day Grace made a campaign appearance in the small town of Louisville, Georgia. In those days, the centerpiece of the town square in Louisville was not a courthouse or a war memorial but an old slave market, a tragic and evil place where human beings had once been bought and sold. Grace chose the slave market as the site for her campaign speech, and as she stood on the very spot where slaves had been auctioned, a hostile crowd of storekeepers and farmers gathered to hear what she would say. "The old has passed away," she began, "and the new has come. This place," she said, gesturing to the market, "represents all about our past over which we must repent. A new day is here, a day when Georgians white and black can join hands to work together."

This was provocative talk in the Georgia of 1962, and the crowd stirred. "Are you a communist?" someone shouted at her.

Grace paused in midsentence. "No," she said softly. "I am not."

"Well, then," continued the heckler, "where'd you get those damned ideas?"

Grace thought for a minute, and then she pointed to the steeple of a nearby church. "I got them over there," she said, "in Sunday school."[29]

The narratives of church, the narratives of scripture, and the narratives of contemporary life told with a theological eye, formed a frame of meaning for Grace Thomas that sent her with hope and determination headlong into the moral fray in a conflicted time.

Because pulpit storytelling is a dress rehearsal for the living of the Christian life, this means that it is ethically irresponsible to tell the canned and simplistic preacher stories that drain away the moral and theological ambiguities inherent in real life. Preacher stories that always yield the right moral lesson or end up in triumph without struggle are a damned lie about human life and Christian faith.

If the preaching of the gospel is, as Calvin would have it, a means by which "the children of Adam and Eve become the children of Christ,"[30] then we will have to tell honestly the storied experiences of both kinds of children, the children of Adam and Eve and the children of Christ, stories of tragedy and stories of hope, stories of conflict and stories of peace. Contemporary sermon stories that are honest about the gains and losses in the moral life, that wrest theological meaning from the midst of ambiguity and struggle, model what Christians are called to do every day in the mundane narratives of life.

2. *Narrative as Congregational Canon.* Sermon stories not only provide a dress rehearsal for the Christian life; they also help to form the working canon of narratives for a congregation. Stanley Hauerwas and

David Burrell have wondered if every one of us does not live out of a set of canonical stories that shape our convictional life.[31] I do know that congregations have sets of canonical narratives, what theologian Michael Welker has called a "living cultural . . . canonic memory [that] connects together a multitude of perspectives on the presence of Christ which are all interdependently related in a continual interplay."[32] At the core are the memories of scripture—memories of God summoning the sun and moon to light the sky, memories of human beings before God, of Sarah laughing and David beating his breast in grief, of Mary pondering these things in her heart and Jesus blessing the children and Paul being shipwrecked. But congregations also add to this biblical core narratives of their own.

I grew up in a small congregation of farmers and teachers in what in those days was rural country outside of Atlanta. One Sunday, in the middle of our worship service, a man we had never seen before burst through the back door of the church. As every eye in the congregation was trained on him, he made his way down the side aisle of the church. Who was he? We were near the tracks of the Southern Railroad, and perhaps he was a drifter who had ridden on the rods of a boxcar. We were beside the highway; maybe he had hitchhiked from the hills to the north. He stared at us, we stared at him. Our minister stopped preaching and stared. He stared back. Suddenly a strange look crossed his face, and he bolted back out the door, never to be seen by us again.

For weeks, after every service, the adults would gather under the trees in the front yard of the church, and they would discuss and debate what had happened. Finally they came to a red-clay-Georgia farmers' theological consensus, and it was not that a vagrant had disrupted our service. It was rather that we had failed some moral test, that God had sent us a stranger and we had not responded as we were called to do.

This experience, this story, became a part of the local canon of our congregation, a reminder of our frailty, and a guide to our ethical life. We did not know, but it would not have surprised us to know, that the Christian church had already added this experience to its narrative canon. As the third-century catechetical document *Didascalia* states: "If a destitute man or woman . . . arrives unexpectedly . . . and there is no place, you, bishop, make such a place with all your heart, even if you yourself should sit on the ground . . . that your ministry may be pleasing before God."[33]

3. *Narrative as a Means for Remembering the Lost and Silenced.* The ethics of pulpit storytelling call on us to add to the church's canon and

to keep alive in the church's memory the stories of those whose lives are not remembered and celebrated and truthfully narrated elsewhere in our culture. Paul Ricoeur has said, "We tell stories because in the last analysis human lives need and merit being narrated. [It is necessary] to save the history of the defeated and the lost. The whole history of suffering . . . calls for narrative."[34]

In an essay on the practice of testimony, theologian Rebecca Chopp tells about Anna Akhmatova, a poet well known in the Soviet Union despite the fact that her poetry was banned for most of her life. In the poem "Requiem," Akhmatova tells about the political imprisonment of her son and of her long days standing with the other mothers and relatives outside the prison. In a prologue to this poem, Akhmatova writes, "In the terrible years of the Yezhov terror I spent seventeen months waiting in line outside the prison in Leningrad. One day somebody in the crowd identified me. Standing behind me was a woman, with lips blue from the cold, who had, of course, never heard me called by name before. Now she stared out of the torpor common to us all and asked me in a whisper (everyone whispered there):

"'Can you describe this?'"

"And I said, 'I can.' Then something like a smile passed fleetingly over what had once been her face."[35]

Can the church, can preaching describe this? We can. Feminist Catholic theologian Elizabeth Johnson connects this narration of the unnarrated with the church's observance of All Saints: "In remembering all saints . . . the church is called to look tragedy in the face. It must recognize the massive, anonymous dead as individual sisters and brothers. . . . It should give voice to the dead, as John Paul II did so dramatically while visiting the Nazi concentration camp in Mauthausen, Austria:

> You people who have experienced fearful torture. . . . What is your last word? . . . You people of yesterday, and you people of today, if the system of extermination camps continues somewhere in the world even today, tell us. . . . Speak, you have the right to do so—you who have suffered and lost your lives. We have the duty to listen to your testimony.[36]

4. *Narrative as a Process for Coming to Faith.* Stories are not just inert containers with ideas inside; they are narrative pathways that beckon readers and hearers on a journey of suspense and discovery. Especially

when it comes to biblical stories, the process of traveling down the narrative corridors can itself be a faith-forming adventure.

In his book *The Poetics of Biblical Narrative*, Meir Sternberg ponders the odd fact that biblical narratives, although they are treasured as guides for the faithful life, are actually not all that straightforward, clear, and easy to read. They are ambiguous and complex, full of fissures, disconnections in the plots, and reading pitfalls. Why? This is not, Sternberg ventures, accidental or superfluous. Instead, these narratives are difficult because of what they are and what they aim to do: texts that summon readers and hearers to see themselves as human beings standing in the presence of God. The sweat and anguish of trying to make sense out of them replicates the very process of coming to faith. Regarding the gaps, non sequiturs, and discontinuities of biblical narratives that form stumbling blocks for the reader, he says:

> With the narrative become an obstacle course, its reading turns into a drama of understanding—conflict between inferences, seesawing, reversal, discovery, and all. The only knowledge perfectly acquired is the knowledge of our limitation. It is by a sustained effort alone that the reader can attain at the end to something of the vision that God has possessed all along: to make sense of the discourse is to gain a sense of being human.[37]

Likewise, in his *The Poetics of Biblical Narrative,* Robert Alter observes that the scriptures were composed by many different authors over a span of several centuries, but even so, they nonetheless roughly form a common literary project, one that seeks "through the process of narrative realization to reveal to the enactment of God's purposes in historical events."[38] So far, so good, then; the scriptures, as a whole, seek to reveal God at work in human history. But in the actual narratives, Alter says, things quickly get complicated—and here he especially echoes Sternberg—because of two sets of tensions that operate throughout scripture: first, the tension between the steadiness of the divine plan and the disorderliness of real human events, and second, the tension between the divine will and human freedom, particularly the stubborn and resistant side of that freedom, what Alter calls "the refractory nature of man." Alter states that "it might be possible to say that the depth with which human nature is imagined in the Bible is a function of its being conceived as caught in the powerful interplay of this double dialectic between design and disorder, providence and freedom."[39]

In a review of Alter's book, Paul Ricoeur extends the argument, maintaining that a faith tradition that has at its heart the interplay of divine providence and human freedom does not just employ the narrative voice, it demands it:

> [The biblical narratives] are not pious stories; they are stories of cunning and murder, stories where the right of primogeniture is scoffed at, where the election of the hero depends upon the oblique maneuvers of an ambitious young man such as David. Taking this problem up from the other end, we might say that a theology that confronts the inevitability of the divine plan with the refractory nature of human plans and actions is a theology that engenders narrative; better it is a theology that calls for the narrative mode as its major hermeneutical mode.

For Ricoeur (and we will explore this in more detail in the next chapter), narratives do more than please us aesthetically or express powerful emotions. They can gather up the bits and pieces of life and "configure" and "refigure" them into a meaningful world of action and purpose. Neurologist Oliver Sacks, in *The Man Who Mistook His Wife for a Hat*, describes a patient of his named Jimmie G., a former sailor who for several decades suffered from Korsakov's syndrome, a brain disease involving severe amnesia. Jimmie lost three decades of memory and could not retain isolated items in his mind for more than a fleeting second. "Do you think he has a soul?" Sacks asked the nuns who cared for him in the nursing facility where he lived. They were outraged by the question. "Watch Jimmie in chapel and judge for yourself," they said. Sacks went to observe Jimmie in the chapel, and reports on what he saw:

> I was moved, profoundly moved and impressed, because I saw here an intensity and steadiness of attention and concentration that I had never seen before in him or conceived him capable of. I watched him kneel and take the Sacrament on his tongue, and could not doubt the fullness and totality of Communion, the perfect alignment of his spirit with the spirit of the Mass. Fully, intensely, quietly, in the quietude of absolute concentration and attention, he entered and partook of the Holy Communion. He was wholly held, absorbed, by a feeling. There was no forgetting, no Korsakov's then, nor did it seem possible that there could be, for he was no longer at the mercy of a faulty and fallible mechanism—that of meaningless sequences and memory traces—but was absorbed in an act, an act of his whole being, which carried feeling and meaning in an organic

continuity and unity, a continuity and unity so seamless it could not permit any break.[40]

Gathered up into the narrative of the Mass, Jimmie's fragmented and episodic life was configured into meaning. He was "no longer fluttering, restless, bored, and lost, but deeply attentive to the beauty and soul of the world."[41]

What has been for the last thirty years called narrative preaching has too often devolved into a hodgepodge of sentimental pseudoart, confused rhetorical strategies, and competing theological epistemologies. Preachers have larded sermons with silly stories of their pets and their children, told anecdotes from the playground to illustrate Golgotha, told hundreds of stories about certain kinds of people and shut out others, and crafted shifty trapdoor plots to keep the listeners amused. If the effect of the recent critiques is to burn away this kind of story stubble, then burn, baby, burn.

But at its best the narrative impulse in preaching grows out of a deep sense of the character, shape, and epistemology of the gospel. If preaching is a sacramental meeting place between the church and the word, the hearers and the gospel, then the substance of preaching is shaped by scripture and by human experience under the sign of grace, and both of these aspects call for narration.

In this way, preaching bears a similarity to the Eucharist. We come from the ambiguities and brokenness of our lives to the Lord's Table, and there we encounter a gracious and benevolent God who gives and gives and gives. When we get up from that Table, our vision has been changed, transfigured, so that we now see the world as it truly is, both in its brokenness and in its character as the theater of the glory of God, to which it is our duty and delight to say, "Thank you, thank you, thank you." Likewise, if we come to the "audible sacrament" of preaching, and there encounter the One who speaks to us the life-giving promises, then it is the task of preaching not only to announce those promises and to reflect on them, but also to imagine what shape a life formed in truthful testimony, just living, and thankful praise might take. Preaching is preparation for people to go to out to Main Street, and to Darfur, and to the neighbor's house, and to the funeral home, living as those who are not afraid to tell the truth about the fractures they see in human experience, because they are also ones who see God's grace and judgment at work in those places.

The giddy season of narrative preaching is coming to an end, and good riddance. None of us is as enchanted by that kind of story sermons as perhaps we once were; none of us is convinced that some-how "narrative saves." We also know that the cycles of homiletical history will surely repeat themselves. At some point in the future, American preaching will once more become stuffy and stale and dog-matic, and when it does, a new generation of preachers will "discover" narrative preaching for the first time—again.

But as for now, a chastened, revised, theologically more astute, and biblically engaged form of narrative preaching endures, and will con-tinue to endure. Perhaps the most reliable measure is whether the life of the church is nourished by such preaching and finds itself more and more formed in the image of Christ. Faithful preaching is not story time; it is instead the spoken word at the epicenter of a community of courageous testimony. Such preaching models the vocabulary, the hos-pitable style of talking, the humility, the prayerful seeking, the aware-ness of ambiguity, the confident hope, and the gospel-storied shape of the lives of people who will talk to their children about their faith and bear witness in the world to the overwhelming generosity of God.

2

No News Is Bad News: God in the Present Tense

When the penny drops, the Bible suddenly becomes three-dimensional rather than a flat, uniform surface.
— John Barton, *The Nature of Biblical Criticism*[1]

One of the best known, and certainly one of the most hotly debated, moments in church history concerns the day that Martin Luther celebrated his first mass as a newly ordained priest. As a Luther biographer, John M. Todd, describes it, the first mass was an exceptionally momentous day for Luther, and getting ready for it was something like preparing for a wedding.[2] On the one hand, Luther approached this first mass profoundly aware that he was now a priest and that this was to be a sacred act of worship. He was determined to remain focused on his liturgical task, detached from all worldly distractions. On the other hand, there were many worldly distractions. A new priest's first mass was a highly public spectacle, a kind of nuptial, graduation party, and debutante ball wrapped into one. There were bright torches and gala feasts and a gaggle of well-wishers, friends, and family, all present to celebrate Martin's debut (including Luther's brooding father Hans, who was still grumpy and displeased that Martin had become a priest). As the moment approached, the 23-year-old Luther was as nervous as a groom, and unfortunately, as Todd observes, "The day itself proved to be, if not exactly a disaster, a day which Luther could not remember without quaking."[3]

What happened? Like most beginning clergy, Luther was terrified he would commit a blunder at the altar, that he would spill the wine or stumble over a prayer, but he made no obvious mistakes. What happened is that he had what we would call a momentary but fairly severe panic attack, a seizure of paralysis and terror. It came just as he raised his voice to speak the Great Prayer in the Canon of the Mass, that long recital of the narrative of the Last Supper, which includes the consecration of the elements. Luther was standing at the high altar, and he began to intone, "Therefore, O most merciful Father . . ." And then it happened. As Todd describes it,

> Suddenly, he was overtaken in a flash by an instant identity crisis. How dare he, how could he actually speak to God? The whole thing was unthinkable. He felt obliterated in the face of the assumption that he was to address God. For a moment he made as if to leave the altar, and said something to the Prior who was standing by him, to assist him at his first Mass, as was the custom, precisely in case the new celebrant experienced any difficulty. The Prior smiled and turned him back to his task. In a moment it was over. From the body of the church, nothing strange would have been noticed— the celebrant with his back to the congregation had to move about from time to time in any case. Martin returned to the text and continued the Mass, sweating and shaken, but safely couched again in the routine.[4]

Luther himself described this meltdown theologically. Kierkegaard once remarked that "Luther always spoke and acted as if lightning were about to strike behind him the next moment."[5] Sure enough, Luther's later description of what happened to him that day is dramatic and electrically charged. When he started into the prayer, he said, "I was utterly stupefied and terror-struck. I thought to myself, 'With what tongue shall I address such Majesty? . . . I am dust and ashes and I am speaking to the living, eternal, and true God!'"[6]

Erik Erikson, however, has famously doubted that it was only Luther's awareness of the majesty of God that turned him into jelly, and suggested that it was also his deeply neurotic psyche. Erikson envisions Luther, standing there facing the high altar with his back to the congregation, as a fragile wisp caught between the pincers of two powerful and frowning fathers: the divine and the earthly. "In front of him," said Erikson, "was the Eucharist's uncertain grace; behind him his father's [i.e., Hans's] potential wrath."[7] The overwhelming and mystic presence of the sacrament combined with an "infantile struggle" over obedience and identification with his father to reduce Luther to a shaking mass of speechless fear.[8]

HIDING FROM THE HOLY MYSTERY

To be honest, as a child of our time and culture, and as one who has himself felt in leading worship the paralyzing fear of stage fright and the sweaty aftershocks of God-knows-what subterranean psychic earthquakes, I am tempted to find Erikson's psychosocial explanation somehow more plausible than Luther's own more theological one. And the fact that I do, and that in doing so I share the widespread assumptions of the current cultural moment, is both interesting and revealing. There is something about me anyway—something about most of us perhaps, something about our time—that can more easily imagine ourselves being awestruck by psychic trauma than by a theophany, can more quickly see ourselves reduced to quivering by our unconscious than by our Creator, can more readily imagine ourselves crumpled to the floor in paralyzed awe by child-hood regression than by the presence of the *mysterium tremendum*.

Years ago, when I was a seminary student, I spent a summer as a pastoral intern in a congregation in the Carolinas. My supervising pastor assigned me the task of visiting and providing pastoral care to several families in the church. One of these families was fairly large, parents and a number of children, the youngest of whom (I will call him Robert) was born with cerebral palsy. When I would visit the family, I would often find them at the dinner table, or gathered in their den, laughing, telling stories, enjoying each other, but not Robert. It was as if the family were bathed in a circle of light—all except for Robert, who stood isolated in the shadows, outside the circle, watching the others.

One day, I happened to be visiting in this home, and only Robert's mother was there. After we chatted for a while, she wanted to tell me about something she had experienced only a few days before. She told me that she had been sitting late in the afternoon in the very room where we were now talking. She was reading or knitting (I can no longer remember), and Robert was standing in the darkness of the hallway, watching her from a distance. She said she felt a strange shift in the room, something that caused her to look up and then down the hallway toward Robert. She told me, "I saw Jesus with his arm around Robert's shoulder." She said she looked away, then back, and there was only Robert. "For the first time since he was born," she said, "I saw my son as already healed in the power of God."

Now I honestly don't know the full truth of what happened there, but I do know the two different reactions that Robert's mother and I had to that experience. She turned the experience into ethics. Because of that visionary moment, she got to work in the community and started several programs in the schools and in the town for kids with disabilities. Some of these programs are still in place, today, decades later. As for me, I had just taken a quarter of clinical pastoral education (a hands-on training program in pastoral care that includes heavy doses of personal analysis and psychology), and, with that course still on my mind, what I did was to psychoanalyze what happened, fortunately silently to myself. "She is feeling so guilty about this child," I told myself, "that she has projected her failings through the symbol system of the Christian faith." In other words, I took an experience she felt she needed theological language to explain and reduced it to psychology so that I could move it around on the chessboard of manageability.

Sociologist of religion Peter Berger has described how the very conditions of scientific, technological society, even when society publicly celebrates religious value, nonetheless subtly pressure people "to soft-pedal if not to abandon altogether" the genuinely transcendent dimensions of religious experience. "Two hypotheses are possible" he says about experiences of God in the midst of life:

> One, that [contemporary people] have such experiences not at all, or at any rate much less frequently than used to be the case in earlier times. Or, two, that [contemporary people] have such experience as much as [people] ever had it, but that because of the delegitimation of that experience by the prevailing worldview, they hide or deny it (the denial, of course, could be to themselves as well as to others).[9]

Every religious experience needs multiple languages to describe it (there are elements in the experience of Robert's mother that can surely best be described psychologically or sociologically), but in our time these languages compete with each other until the language of the transcendent is defeated and replaced by more proximate and reasonable explanations. This process, the transcendent gradually giving way to the exclusively immanent, is sometimes given the broad label "secularity," and it is viewed as inevitable, inexorable, and sometimes even as a very good thing. The result is that many people, especially educated people, are persuaded that visions of Jesus in the hallway, while perhaps understandable and certainly meaningful to the people who imagine them, must evaporate in the clear light of rationality. Such experiences can be better understood and be even more meaningful, when, like

Erikson's assessment of Luther's moment of dread at the altar, they are reframed in languages less distorting than the language of religious piety. The argument, put simply, is that the rational and scientific worldviews that characterize advanced societies provide the means for a clearing of our vision, wiping away the distortions of magical thinking and religious myth, allowing what has always been truly there in the universe and in human nature to come into the clear light.

Philosopher Charles Taylor names this way of describing secularism a "subtraction story," by which he means that "natural" and immanent ways of framing life inevitably shove "supernatural" and transcendent views off the scene, thus subtracting them from the equation. The idea is that every human being and every society needs an essential way to make sense of the world, and that when societies progress toward a new and more adequate worldview, the previous worldview must fold its hand, cash in its chips, and leave the table. Allegiance to the subtraction story is, by the way, the common coin in the recent spate of popular attack books written by professed atheists, who are both outraged and bewildered by the fact that billions of people on the planet stubbornly cling to some form of religious faith in the face of four centuries of scientific progress, which should have convinced the whole human race to toss out all vestiges of faith like poodle skirts and Nehru jackets. Literary critic Terry Eagleton, in a witty and scathing review of one of those books, Richard Dawkins's *The God Delusion*, notes,

Dawkins holds that the existence or non-existence of God is a scientific hypothesis which is open to rational demonstration. Christianity teaches that to claim that there is a God must be reasonable, but that this is not at all the same thing as faith. Believing in God, whatever Dawkins might think, is not like concluding that aliens or the tooth fairy exist. God is not a celestial super-object or divine UFO, about whose existence we must remain agnostic until all the evidence is in. Theologians do not believe that he is either inside or outside the universe, as Dawkins thinks they do. His transcendence and invisibility are part of what he is, which is not the case with the Loch Ness monster. This is not to say that religious people believe in a black hole, because they also consider that God has revealed himself: not, as Dawkins thinks, in the guise of a cosmic manufacturer even smarter than Dawkins himself . . . but for Christians at least, in the form of a reviled and murdered political criminal. The Jews of the so-called Old Testament had faith in God, but this does not mean that after debating the matter at a number of international conferences they decided to endorse the scientific hypothesis that there existed a supreme architect of the universe—even though, as Genesis reveals, they were of this opinion. They had faith in God in the sense that I have faith in you. They may well have been mistaken in their view; but they were not mistaken because their scientific hypothesis was unsound.[10]

Taylor, albeit from a somewhat different angle than Eagleton, also disputes the prevailing subtraction accounts. Rather than seeing secularity as the tale of how scientific rationalism inescapably erases older religious accounts of life, Taylor sees it, to the contrary, as a kind of addition story. "Against this kind of [subtraction] story," he writes in the beginning of *A Secular Age*, "I will steadily be arguing that Western modernity, including its secularity, is the fruit of new inventions, newly constructed self-understandings and related practices, and can't be explained in terms of perennial features of human life."[11] Religious faith, as Taylor would describe it, is not the automatic victim of the Enlightenment, destined to obsolescence as scientific rationalism marches in to take its place, but religious accounts of life must now compete in the marketplace of ways of understanding the world. Belief in God is neither impossible nor irrational in the glare of modernity, but it "is no longer axiomatic. There are alternatives."[12]

LOSING OUR MOTHER TONGUE

We who preach have learned so many languages to express what we are doing—whether we are giving people inspiration or building up the church or serving as social critics or providing positive role models. Yet I wonder if we have lost our mother tongue. If there are, as Taylor says, alternatives, how clearly are we announcing the alternative that is the gospel? To be sure, preachers are not supposed to confine themselves only to the "language of Zion," as if we were befuddled tourists from a remote island with its own obscure language, who have suddenly stepped off a bus in New York City and are now waving our hands in the air and jabbering away, trying to make ourselves understood. In the Christian faith, which has as a central claim that "the Word became flesh and lived among us" (John 1:14), preaching is compelled to be a multilingual activity, mixing theological terms and scriptural accounts with the artifacts of culture—scenes from films and novels, snatches of dialogue from television and advertisements, bits from the blogosphere and ideas drawn from the fields of science, history, politics, and psychology. And this mingling of the language of the faith with elements from the culture is not simply to make the sermon "interesting" or "relevant to today." Rather preaching acts out what it means for Christian faith to be set down in the welter of worldviews, convictions, and counterclaims of society.

Preaching, like the gospel it proclaims, ventures out into the crowded public square and heralds its news, establishes dialogue, engages in debate, finds common ground, explains itself, defends its convictions, forms friendships, calls for repentance both inside and outside the community of faith, tells its story, and embodies hospitality to the stranger. In short, preaching, which most usually takes place as a moment in worship inside the walls of a church, models the exciting, confusing, high-stakes, polyglot encounter that takes place when serious Christians go into the world as disciples of Christ, prepared to bear witness to their faith and to listen to the deep stories of others in the roiling marketplace of ideas, behaviors, and truth claims that makes up our world. What Christians are called to do every day in the world, preaching does paradigmatically in the theater of worship: negotiate a hearing for the faith in, with, and for the world.

The playing field is not level, of course. Preachers who have misunderstood or willfully distorted the gospel, preachers with small-minded and mean-spirited versions of the Christian faith, have scorched the earth before us, and gospel preachers must now proceed assuming that, for far too many hearers, the words of grace, wonder, and joy that form the vocabulary of the faith now sound like the harsh language of an invading army. Moreover, versions of the "subtraction story" have taken root in the popular mind, forcing many thoughtful people to wonder if being a person of faith is foolish in a scientific age. Out of loyalty to clear-headed, scientific thinking, they put away the "childish things" of faith and walk away, albeit with a wistful backward glance. "[T]oday, . . ." writes Charles Taylor,

> when a naturalistic materialism is not only an offer, but presents itself as the only view compatible with the most prestigious institution of the modern world, viz., science; it is quite conceivable that one's doubts about one's own faith, about one's ability to be transformed, or one's sense of how one's own faith is childish and inadequate, could mesh with this powerful ideology, and send one off along the path of unbelief, even though with regret and nostalgia.[13]

Negotiating a hearing for the faith means, of course, speaking clearly and boldly, among the several languages we employ, the one language specially entrusted to our care, the language of the gospel, the language of what the God we know in Jesus Christ through the Holy Spirit has done, is doing, and will do among us.

Oddly, though, this is the language that seems most missing from much current preaching. Yes, there is plenty of God-talk and religious chatter in the pulpit today, but what seems absent is the vibrant sense of the living divine reality, the holy presence that almost sent Luther fleeing from the chancel. Perhaps this is an overly harsh judgment, but listen to sermons being preached these days in the broad mainline churches, and see if they do not often have the hollow sound of an old oak whose living center has died and rotted away. Yes, yes, there are sincere words about God and the "power of our faith," that sort of thing, but frequently it all seems to come as an act of nostalgia, with a cool detachment from the possibility that the sermon itself might be caught up in the event of revelation, and accompanied by the tacit admission that, really, when we get down to it, whatever good there is in life is the product of our own industry and intention, that when all is said and done, this world is all we have and we are the only ones in here. As one of my keenest students complained, the sermons she had heard were often "like listening to something on National Public Radio: well researched, very well written prose, clever and witty in places, well voiced, but oral religious essays, nevertheless."

This lack of attention to the presence of God is not, I think, a matter of lack of faith or willful neglect on the part of most preachers. Almost every Christian preacher desires to speak the gospel, to bear witness to God's presence and action in the world. What has happened to the pulpit is more like a habit of speech, being accommodated to the way our culture uses religious language, namely, as holy sounding talk with all the edges filed away, so that it refers not to the wild, undomesticated presence of the living God, but only to us, to our sincere hearts, spiritual intentions, and our desire to do good things in life. In other words, there is plenty of morality and good counsel, but no desert bush bursting into flame.

There was a great moment when Frederick Douglass was addressing a Boston audience about racism in America, and Sojourner Truth was there in the auditorium, sitting, tall and attentive, on the very front row, facing the platform. Douglass grew more and more agitated, more and more despairing as he spoke, saying finally that there was no hope for justice outside of violence and bloodshed. When Douglass sat down, the hall fell into a tense hush. Then in her deep and commanding voice, Sojourner Truth spoke a sentence heard all over the room: "Frederick, is God dead?"

Whenever I tune into the overly upbeat television preachers or, closer to home, run into the casual, chatty preachers of the relaxed suburban congregation, welcoming people with the perkiness of a TV weathercaster and running through the joys and concerns as if they were the recreational program directions of a cruise ship, I recall what Karl Barth said about preaching to a gathering of ministers one summer day many years ago, and my heart beats faster. He was talking about what he called "the great peril" of preaching, and he said,

> What are you doing, you [human being], with the Word of *God* upon *your* lips? Upon what grounds do you assume the role of mediator between heaven and earth? Who has authorized you to take your place there and to generate religious feeling? . . . *Is* not the whole situation in the church an illustration of [humanity's] chronic presumption . . . ? Can a minister be saved? I would answer that with [humans] this is impossible; but with God all things *are* possible. *God* may pluck us as a brand out of the fire. But so far as *we* know, there is no one who deserves the wrath of God more abundantly than the ministers.[14]

The fearsome idea that preachers might indeed take the Word of God on their lips is at the root of the story told about an old Welsh pastor who preached every Sunday in a pulpit at the top of a winding staircase. Every Sunday, the aged minister would struggle slowly up those steps to preach. One Sunday, however, he started up the stairs, but halfway up halted and suddenly, as if paralyzed with fear, shouted into the air, "I will not . . . I will NOT go into that awful place." But then, a moment of frozen silence, he lifted his foot and climbed obediently into the pulpit to preach. Now I have no interest in increasing the anxiety of preaching. It is high enough as it is. I would be dismayed if every Sunday I had to wrestle with a Luther-style panic attack, or stood in the pulpit with Barthian abject humiliation, or wondered if lightning were about to strike behind me at any moment. However, what I find exhilarating in Paul and Luther and Barth and Sojourner Truth and others like them is the profound awareness that we are not finally left to our own devices, that something powerful and holy is about to happen in the event of preaching, and that this eventfulness is gathered into the language of the sermon.

I am well aware of the dangers on the other side of the coin, namely, those preachers who rattle on as if they were God's press secretaries, chatting with all the blithe confidence of court insiders about what God is doing, saying, thinking, wanting, and feeling today. We would do well to remind ourselves that scripture tells us not only of a God who is present to us through acting, speaking, and responding in life, but also of a God who is present by being hidden, withdrawn, and silent, indeed a God whose "face," were it to become too near and completely visible, would destroy us (Exod. 33:20).

This is why seeing God's hand at work in our world and the ability to name this in preaching comes as a gift, and not as an achievement. It comes through prayer and the expectant study of scripture, not as the by-product of some system of theology that has God's ways and will figured out. This is also why Paul says of his own preaching that, on the one hand, he proclaimed "the mystery of God" and that it was accompanied by "a demonstration of the Spirit and of power," but that, on the other hand, Paul himself came to them in "weakness and in fear and in much trembling," and his sermons were not woven out of "plausible words of wisdom." It's not that preachers already know what God is up to in the world; we don't. But when preachers open themselves up to the Spirit and are given a glimpse of God's action in the world, of the mystery of God, with trembling lips they bear witness to this, so that "faith might not rest on human wisdom but on the power of God" (1 Cor. 2:1–5). As George Stroup has written,

> When Christians speak of the presence of God, they are not simply describing a permanent feature of the "everyday" world. There are moments, events, occasions, when people do experience the presence of God, but this presence is not a reality that is perpetually "at hand." It is not an event in which one suddenly notices something that has always been there but had previously escaped one's attention.[15]

The presence of God is not a commodity to be packaged in a sermon. It is an event to which we give testimony. There is a beautiful scene in Garrett Keizer's *A Dresser of Sycamore Trees*. Keizer, a minister in Vermont, tells of conducting a Saturday night Easter Vigil service in his little church. This is the first time, as far as he can remember, that his parish has observed the Saturday vigil, and only two other people, a husband and wife, have shown up for the service. Keizer lights the paschal candle and begins the liturgy: "Dear friends in Christ: On this most holy night, in which our Lord Jesus passed over from death to life, the Church invites her members, dispersed throughout the world to gather in vigil and prayer." The candle sputters in the half darkness, Keizer writes,

> like a voice too embarrassed or overwhelmed to proclaim the news: "Christ is risen."
>
> But it catches fire, and there we are, three people and a flickering light in an old church on a Saturday evening in the spring, with the noise of the cars and their winter rusted mufflers outside. The moment is filled with the ambiguities of all such quiet observances among few people, in the midst of an oblivious population in a radically secular age. The act is so ambiguous because its terms are so extreme: the Lord is with us, or we are pathetic fools. I like it that way. I believe God likes it that way. My worry is always that others will be discouraged rather than exalted by the omnipresence of the two possibilities.[16]

The Lord is with us, or we are pathetic fools. I like it that way too. To put it in preaching terms, either God is present and active in our preaching, or we are poseurs and pathetic fools. We preachers are either fools for Christ or just damned fools: two awesome and awe-ful possibilities, and we just have to take the risk. This is no mere rhetorical ploy. If we do not seriously raise the possibility and run the risk of just being a damn fool, then we will never get near the possibility of being a fool for Christ. I suggest that many preachers today have shied away from these two terrifying possibilities to construct a third and safer option. Much preaching in our day has taken on the posture of Wisdom literature. Take a romp through the thousands of church Web sites on the Internet and sample a sermon here and a sermon there, and what one finds is actually going on in pulpits across the land—at least in pulpits in churches with means enough to maintain Web sites—is an abundance of sage advice. There is sermon wisdom about parenting and wisdom about managing one's money and wisdom about finding purpose in one's work and relationships and wisdom about engaging in the struggle for justice and wisdom about being more caring toward others and wisdom about accepting differences and being more inclusive and wisdom about the doctrinal truths of the faith and wisdom about the biblical texts for the day and wisdom about nurturing one's spiritual life.

We need wisdom, of course; wisdom is an important biblical motif, and some of this pulpit wisdom is sound and mostly Christian, I suppose. But true biblical wisdom is less about life skills and the management of problems than it is a seeking of the shape of faithful living that results from an encounter with the living God. Biblical wisdom is grounded not merely in common sense or in the brilliance of some sage, but in holy encounter. "The fear of the LORD is the beginning of knowledge" (Prov. 1:7). In *Christian Wisdom,* theologian David F. Ford draws the connection between the desire for wisdom and the actions of God:

> *The theological wisdom of faith is grounded in being affirmed, being commanded, being questioned and searched, being surprised and opened to new possibilities, and being desired and loved.* . . . The longing for God, and the passion for realizing the truth, love, justice and peace of God, are together at the heart of the Christian desire for a wisdom that responds with discernment both to the cries of God and to the cries of the world.[17]

Much pulpit wisdom, however, seems to owe less to the paths of life that are trod in breathless wonder on our way back from worship and more to the well-trod lanes of conventional wisdom. Where is the present-tense announcement of God's action in our midst? Where are we, to use Ford's terms again, surprised, questioned, affirmed, commanded, or loved? Sermons on "Five Ways to Keep Your Marriage Alive" or "Keys to a Successful Prayer Life" or even "Standing Up for Peace in a Warring World" may possess some ethical wisdom and some utilitarian helpfulness, but they often have the sickly sweet aroma of smoldering incense in a temple from which the deity has long since departed. They can easily have the sound of the lonely wisdom of Job's friends, who can quote the Psalms and the Proverbs but who have ceased to expect the whirlwind. They are what is left when the possibility of holy encounter has been eliminated and all that remains is how to use religion to manage and cope with our lives and to construct a good life out of the rubble at hand. As for being the good news, many of these sermons are "good," but there's no news, nothing is happening, no event of God erupts, and when it comes to the gospel, *no news is bad news.*

In an oft-quoted remark, Annie Dillard once observed that if we truly understood what was going on in worship, we would wear crash helmets and ushers would lash us to the pews "for the sleeping God may someday awake and take offense."[18] But these wisdom sermons are preached by men and women who have lost the sense of worship's perilous heights and who have been lulled into forgetting that lightning might strike behind them at any moment. Here are sermons, ironically, in which God, as Frederick Buechner once observed, "is the most missed of all missing persons."

By contrast, the Jesuit William Harmless in his book *Augustine and the Catechumenate* has taken us inside the basilica in the ancient North African town of Hippo to recreate the excitement and eventfulness of services where Augustine was the preacher.[19] As Harmless describes these services, they crackled with energy and expectation and presence. In Augustine's mouth, the Word was not merely being taught; in the power of the Spirit, it was flashing in an electric blue arc across the assembly.

Augustine preached at least four times a week, sometimes every day,[20] and the room was crowded with the townspeople standing shoulder to shoulder, "artisans and fishermen, merchants and magistrates," the baptized and the learners, curious pagans, Jews, Donatists, and Manichees, crowding in to hear the magnetic and engaging preacher.[21] But what they heard, Augustine insisted, was not a celebrated orator, but the Word, in a chorus of voices from the cantor, from the reader, from the preacher, in the cries of the assembly. They heard the Word sung and cheered and preached and prayed. "God speaks," said Augustine of the whole worship, "all of this is the voice of God [echoing] throughout the round world."

Now admittedly, Augustine was, his contemporaries confessed, a born preacher and a dazzling orator. Even his harshest critics had to admire his ability to fashion cathedrals out of words. One of Harry Emerson Fosdick's detractors once said, "That man says what I don't believe better than anybody I have ever heard." This was so, for some, with Augustine. For example, Secundicus, a Manichee and a contemporary of Augustine, once quipped about Augustine that he had never been able "to discern a Christian in him, but on all occasions, a born orator, a god of eloquence."[22]

Part of Augustine's effectiveness as a preacher came in the strength of his thought and the simple elegance of his language. He never resorted to the common language of the street. Peter Brown notes that he used the refined Latin of the educated elite, but pared down to an accessible simplicity, so that what sounded like a "superbly unaffected 'Christian' style," says Brown, was actually a "simplicity achieved on the other side of sophistication."[23] But words and ideas alone did not account for the power of his sermons. They were events; something was happening when Augustine preached. His friend Possidius once remarked that people receive much from what Augustine has written, but, how much more have those received who see and hear him preach.[24]

No one could be passive while listening to one of Augustine's sermons, and churchgoing in Hippo was, Harmless says, "a raucous, noisy

affair."[25] The congregation applauded, shouted, cried out. Once in a
sermon Augustine, almost offhandedly, described a man who was traveling to a foreign land to get married but encountered a roaring lion on
the way and strangled it. "Samson, Samson, Samson," his congregation
cried out with delight.[26] Sometimes when Augustine headed off toward
a favorite preaching theme, the hearers would guess where he was going
and encourage him with shouts of anticipation. Or if the scripture
reading or the sermon chastised them in any way, the people would
groan loudly and beat their breasts. "Often," Harmless says, "they
applauded [Augustine's] musical turns of phrase, much as we might
applaud a jazz clarinet's improvisational flurries."[27] This was early
North African call and response.

Here, for example, is a paragraph, a musical riff, in one of Augustine's sermons. As he spoke and the waves of these words broke across
the assembly, the hearers began to ride the waves, cheering with increasing volume and intensity:

> Loved is the world: but let [your love] prefer the One by
>   whom the world was made.
> Vast is the world; but more vast is the One by whom the
>   world was made
> Beautiful is the world; but more beautiful is the One
>   by whom the world was made.
> Alluring is the world; but more alluring is the One
>   by whom the world was made.[28]

By the time he spoke this line, the cheering was so loud that Augustine stopped the sermon in surprise. "What have I said?" he shouted
back to the congregation. "What is there to cheer about? We are still
battling with the problem and you have already started to cheer."

The point here is that something was happening in the event of the
sermon. This is not just reflective wisdom, not even just good oratory.
This is language summoned and swept into the event of God's speaking
and acting. Despite his classical training in the rules of oratory, Augustine believed that being caught up in the event of the preached Word
generated its own kind of eloquence, an eloquence parallel to the eloquence of scripture itself. This, said Augustine, is an eloquence that,
like "wisdom proceeding out of her own home," springs naturally from
its subject.[29] "When I unpack the . . . scripture," Augustine said in a
sermon, "I [am] breaking open bread for you. What I [give] you is not
mine. What you eat, I eat. What you live on, I live on."[30] "Why do I

preach? Why do I sit up here? What do I live for?" he asked in another sermon. His answer? "For this one thing alone: that together we may live with Christ! This is my passion, this is my honor, this is my fame, this is my joy, this is my one possession!"[31]

RENEWING VISION, RECOVERING VOICE

So while I do not wish for preachers to freeze in panic at the altar, I would hope for preaching today to gain a deeper participation in the eventfulness of God. Part of this will involve recovering a confidence in the capacity of language to be the carrier wave for divine encounter or, perhaps better to say, trust that God will in freedom choose to be present in our little words. Literary critic George Steiner, in his book *Real Presences*, notes the underlying skepticism in our culture that holds the view that when we speak of God, we really do so in the same obsolete way that we speak of "sunrise" and "sunset." In this view, says Steiner, we speak

as if the Copernican model of the solar system had not replaced, ineradicably, the Ptolemaic. Vacant metaphors, eroded figures of speech, inhabit our vocabulary and grammar. They are caught, tenaciously, in the scaffolding and recesses of our common parlance. There they rattle about like old rags or ghosts in the attic.

This is the reason why rational men and women, particularly in the scientific and technological realities of the West, still refer to "God." . . . [God] is a phantom of grammar, a fossil embedded in the childhood of rational speech. So Nietzsche (and many after him).[32]

But Steiner wishes to argue the reverse. He "proposes that any coherent understanding of what language is and how language performs, that any coherent capacity of human speech to communicate meaning and feeling, is, in the final analysis, underwritten by the assumption of God's presence. . . . [W]hen the human voice addresses another, . . . when we encounter the other in its condition of freedom, [it] is a wager on transcendence."[33]

Yes . . . "a wager on transcendence." The preacher, Frederick Buechner reminds us, "deals out [the sermon] note cards like a riverboat gambler. The stakes have never been higher." This is a wager on transcendence. In a review in the *New Yorker* of a volume of literary criticism of the Bible, Steiner admired much of the scholarship and many of the insights, but he finally complains that the authors objectify the biblical text in ways that drain it of both its terror and its numinous power. The Psalms become mere poetry, as Chartres becomes a mere example of architecture, and, he writes, "[L]ike an unplayed Stradivarius, the once-holy text inhabits the air-conditioned case of dispassionate regard."[34] At one point in the review, he says,

> I can—just—come to imagine for myself that a man of more or less my own biological and social composition could have written "Hamlet" or "Lear" and gone home to lunch and found a normal answer to the question, "How did it go today?" I cannot conceive the author of the Speech Out of the Whirlwind in Job writing or dictating that text and dwelling within common existence and parlance.[35]

In addition to a confidence in language as a medium for the Holy, the regaining of a sense of the presence and action of God in preaching also involves a rethinking of a fairly routine and often neglected aspect of sermon preparation, namely, the way we exegete and interpret biblical texts. Just as the finest of cuisines in the grandest of restaurants begins in the kitchen with spices and vegetables and a raw chicken, the sermon in which the windy possibility of transcendence ruffles our hair begins with the day labor of biblical exegesis.

Before I launch into this proposal on exegesis, let me hasten to say that I mean here to add to the preacher's repertoire of approaches to biblical interpretation, not to replace or narrow them. Preaching is odd business, when we think about it. We stand up, week after week in a highly visible place holding a several-thousand-year-old text and commit acts of public hermeneutics, and that takes nimbleness, imagination, creativity, and every responsible method we can get our hands on. I will never forget, some years ago, reading the breathtaking explorations of biblical texts in the book *Text and Texture*[36] by Rabbi Michael Fishbane, now professor of Jewish studies at the University of Chicago Divinity School. There Fishbane does what he calls "close readings" of a couple dozen biblical texts, and the results are stunning. His methods are various: sometimes he uses historical criticism, sometimes he is the literary critic; here he uses sociology, there Jewish mysticism. It is all seamless; one cannot tell when he moves from one method to the other, and the texts yield one moving insight after another. I was quite surprised to read sometime later another biblical scholar's review of Fishbane's work. He placed Fishbane essentially as a literary critic but then sniffed that Fishbane "does not propose any general critical method . . . and [the book] seems finally less concerned with poetics than with homiletics."[37] Less concerned with poetics than with *homiletics*? It was not a compliment. What the critic meant was that Fishbane, for all of his skill, finally stained his methodological purity for the sake of the highly lamentable desire to say something from these texts that faithful people just might find worth hearing. He was "merely homiletical." It is true, of course. Fishbane uses many methods, not just one, and that is because the driving force for him, I think, is finally that he is a rabbi, that at the end of the day there is a congregation of people waiting for him, people who want to live their real lives in the light of these texts.

Herb Gardner, the playwright, once confessed that his recurring anxiety dream is that he is writing the last act of a new play. But he is not quietly at his desk in his study. He is sitting at a folding table on the stage of the Booth Theater in New York writing furiously, and on the other side of the curtain he can hear the audience gathering. People are taking their seats, folding their playbills, coughing, and chatting. In a few minutes the curtain will rise, and the play is not finished.

I can identify powerfully with that anxiety dream. It is Sunday morning, and I can hear the congregation gathering, coughing and folding their bulletins, and the sermon is not finished. There I am in the study with a suddenly recalcitrant text. At the beginning of the week, it seemed like such a nice little passage, all sweet and chatty, but now it has turned cold and surly on me. Will I use every method I know? You can be sure I will. I will pry it with the crowbar of historical criticism. I will entreat it with rhetorical categories and sociology and feminism and liberation thought. I will get down on my knees and beg, "Speak to me that I may speak." Because in a few minutes the curtain will rise, and they will be out there, and they will be, in ways they sometimes don't even know, asking me the question shouted out by many African American congregations: "Is there a Word from the Lord?" Forgive me, then, my methodological promiscuity. I am but a preacher, a beggar, and my needs are "merely homiletic."

So how can exegesis bring our preaching closer to the eventfulness of God? In his fascinating book *Preaching Paul*, New Testament scholar Daniel Patte explored, not how to preach the Pauline Epistles, but what we can learn about preaching in our day by examining Paul's own preaching methodology. Paul, argued Patte, was in a cultural situation much like our own. He had a gospel to preach that was couched in a vocabulary his hearers did not know—Jewish apocalyptic. He was preaching to people whose language and thought forms were shaped by culture other than the gospel, namely, Hellenism. So what should he do? Should he ask the Hellenists to learn the Jewish apocalyptic concepts, risking befuddlement? Or should he attempt to translate Jewish apocalyptic thought into their categories, into Hellenistic philosophical terms, risking losing something essential about the gospel in translation? Paul, claims Patte, chose a third option. Paul instead held the Jewish apocalyptic gospel like a lens to the eye of his imagination and looked through it toward his culture. He looked at the world of his hearers through the cross-resurrection refraction of the gospel, and by doing so, he saw something he could not have seen without the gospel lens: the trajectory of God in their world. He saw God at work in cross-resurrection ways in their present-tense circumstances, and he told them what he saw. God is present; God is at work in your world. Can you see it? "Preaching Paul's gospel," claimed Patte, "is essentially the proclamation that the power of God for salvation is at work in our present. . . . The power of the Gospel is manifested for us NOT when we learn a general principle, but when we are confronted by Christ-like manifestations of God in our midst."[38]

What Patte is doing here offers a hermeneutical option to the preacher that is both more complex and more powerful than the customary attempt to find simple analogies between the text and our context, a sermon technique that tells a story about Jesus or reprises the situation at Corinth, and then announces to the congregation, "Aren't we today just like those Pharisees!" or "Isn't it true that the church in our time is just like that Corinthian congregation?" Well, no, as a matter of fact, we *aren't* just like those Pharisees, and, as a matter of strict historical analogy, the circumstances at ancient Corinth are quite distant from any twenty-first-century setting. Some form of analogical thinking is involved in all hermeneutics, but the connection between text and sermon needs to move beyond the illusion of a tight analogy between the text and our context and toward a more imaginative way to see connections.

Patte goes a long way toward helping us to reclaim the impact of news in our preaching by saying that preaching involves looking through the lenses of biblical texts to discover and then to announce present-tense manifestations of God in the experience of hearers. Patte's view of exegesis is in key ways an elaboration of Calvin's metaphor of the scripture as "spectacles." Commenting on that metaphor, Garrett Green observes, "The scriptures are not something we look *at*, but rather look *through*, lenses that refocus what we see into an intelligible pattern."[39]

But we should not, I think, be fully satisfied with Patte's description of that intelligible pattern. His rather strict structuralism, with its mathematical ensemble of either-or binary oppositions, tends, I think, to restrict the range of patterns found in scripture. For Patte, everything is squeezed through the master binary opposition he finds in Paul: cross-resurrection. Raising the crucified to new life may work as a macro statement of God's action in the world, but when we get closer to the grain, we need more images, more metaphors, more plot structures to describe the full range of God's action in the world. God is blessing and judging, healing and guiding, lifting up the weak and bringing down the oppressor. To view life through scripture, we need a more complex set of lenses than just the one master lens, cross-resurrection.

A wider ranging possibility for biblical preaching is given to us in the narrative hermeneutics of Paul Ricoeur. In *Time and Narrative*, Ricoeur brilliantly and perhaps surprisingly sets Augustine and Aristotle into a conversation about time and plot.[40] There is a long argument to be made here, but that will have to yield to a long story made very short. From Augustine's famous exploration of the nature of time in *The Confessions*, Ricoeur draws a picture of the human being both caught in the fragmented, mysterious, ever-passing-away present tense (there are only three categories of time, thought Augustine, and all of them in the present tense: "a present of past things, a present of present things, and a present of future things") and yet impinged upon by eternity in which, as Augustine says, "there is neither past nor future, [and yet it] determines both past and future time." From Augustine, then, there is the notion of the concordance of things eternal being constantly ripped apart in life lived in an ever-eroding present. In short, for Augustine, life is discordance.

From Aristotle's *Poetics*, Ricoeur draws quite the opposite understanding. If, for Augustine, human life in time is about concordance being shredded into discordance, for Aristotle, the creation of literary plots is about discordance being shaped into concordance. How does literary plot create concord out of discord? Through the process of *mimesis*, the way a storyteller or a poet creatively imitates and synthesizes purposeful human action. In literary *mimesis* an author writes a piece of fiction, but the fiction is drawn from and imitates real life, and this imitation of life is part of the power and appeal of the fiction. For example, the television show *Seinfeld* was a popular hit for years, not simply because it included funny jokes and situations played out by skillful actors, but mainly because it re-presented *mimetically*, that is to say it imitated, a form of life recognizable to its audience: the savvy, somewhat rootless, detached postmodern existence of young urban professionals.

So what happens, according to Ricoeur, when we bring Augustine's discordance into contact with Aristotle's concordance? Here Ricoeur freely, creatively, and I think brilliantly departs from Aristotle's one level of *mimesis* to describe three levels of *mimesis*, which he somewhat playfully calls *mimesis1, mimesis2,* and *mimesis3.*

Mimesis1 is, in effect, life as we experience it and is thus closest to Augustine's discordance. We go through our daily existence, humming along at the level of *mimesis1.* We get dressed, fix the coffee, go to work, wave at a friend across the hall, turn on the computer, start the workday. It doesn't feel like a coherent narrative; it doesn't seem organized or profoundly meaningful. It just seems like the bits and pieces of discordant life (one is reminded of Galen Strawson's description of the Episodic, discussed in the previous chapter). But even though life at the level of *mimesis1* is a cluster of shards and fragments, nevertheless all of the ingredients for a narrative are in place. Indeed, like a person who places vague dream sequences, disconnected bits, and jagged-edged experiences before a psychiatrist, or like a lawyer who articulates partial and contested chucks of evidence before a judge,[41] there is an "untold story" toward which all is leaning, yearning. There are actors, there is action, and there are motives, partial and fragmented though they be. This is *mimesis1*—a narrative lurking beneath the rippled surface, a narrative ready to happen.

The event of preaching to a congregation begins, in one sense, at *mimesis1.*[42] The preacher and the congregation are present together in a room, speaking and listening. The motives, mixed. The experiences, somewhat fragmentary, gapped, and mysterious. Even as the preacher speaks and others hear, this present moment on which all are standing is constantly slipping out from under their feet. A sentence is spoken, and then it is instantly gone, having disappeared into the nothingness of the past. And yet, for all the fragmentation, temporal erosion, and mystery, there is still the tacit sense that this is not absurd, that preacher and hearers are living out some kind of meaningful narrative. All of the ingredients are here—human agency, purpose, potential relationships; its coherence is not fully visible. It is an incipient narrative waiting to be born, but not yet birthed. Ricoeur calls this *mimetic1* condition, this almost-but-not-quite narrative, "prefiguration."

But then the preacher introduces into the equation a biblical text—narrative or narrative-like—and perhaps other stories. These narratives have plots; they imitate, organize, and arrange human action in a coherent way. This is *mimesis2*, and the interaction between *mimesis2* and *mimesis1* Ricoeur calls "configuration." What happens to us when a narrative text intrudes into our consciousness, when *mimesis1* is invaded by *mimesis2*? Ricoeur is convinced—and he has claimed this throughout his career—that a text projects a world of meaning in front of it and beckons us to enter, engage, and be transformed by the encounter with that world. This is controversial, because what Ricoeur is claiming is that texts reliably refer to realities outside themselves, that there really is something "outside the text." He argued this point with Levi-Strauss; he argued this point with the structuralists; he argued this point with Derrida. "[F]or me," he said, "the world is the whole set of references opened by every sort of descriptive or poetic text I have read, interpreted, and loved."[43] I think Ricoeur is right and the nonreferentialists wrong, but, of course, you pay your money and take your choice.

So the discordant shards, fragments, and bits of life at *mimesis1* are brought into the arena of story, into the realm of *mimesis2*, where there is coherence, plot, pattern, sequence, and arrangement. *Mimesis2* brings order out of the disarray of *mimesis1*. But if this interaction were all there is, if the power of narrative were only about ordering that which is disordered, then it would be an unsatisfactory, even dangerous aspect of preaching. Preaching would be about using scripture to create lock-step conformity. Unfortunately, some approaches to biblical preaching seem content to stay at the level of ordering that which is disordered. The implication is that the goal of the preacher is to impose (or, in softer versions, to invite hearers to accept) the order of the biblical narrative upon the disorder of the world. Preachers are to say, in effect, "Now I know you have come here this morning with your lives fragmented and in pieces, but here is the biblical story, which, if you trust it and take it as your story, will order your life and give it coherence."

Ricoeur recognizes that to see the ultimate function of narrative in this way, as only imposing concord upon discord, is asking for trouble. First, there is the trouble of bitter disappointment. If the purpose of the biblical and other sermon narratives is simply to generate conformity, to straighten out the discord of life, then preaching will eventually be viewed as an act of deception and treachery. At the end of the sermon, at the close of the service, people must get up and go back out into the fragmented world of *mimesis1*, and the coherence of the narrative world of *mimesis2* will inevitably seem to them to have been a temporary illusion. Sure, the world of the Bible, the world of the sermon story, is ordered. In that world, captives are released, storms are stilled, the blind see, the dead are raised, unbelief finds reasons for faith, and the kingdom of God is at hand—but not here, not in the real world, not in my world.

Second, there is the trouble of rebellion against authoritarianism. If the job of sermon narrative, biblical and otherwise, is perceived to be like that of the vice principal of the high school, always getting the messy details of life to stand up straight and get in line, then ultimately this will foster rebellion against the heavy handedness of the sermon and the scripture. Indeed, it is a characteristic of our culture to resist imposed authority, and part of modernity's revolt against authority can be seen in its fascination with the unformed, whether in social relationships that have porous and open boundaries, in the literary trend toward the antinarrative novel, or in the desire for a spirituality without the constraints of creed, scripture, sermon, or church (we will run into this hunger for unformed spirituality again in the next chapter, when we examine the new gnosticism in the church).

For Ricoeur, however, narrative works in a more complex way than simply bringing order to disorder. To begin with, the world of *mimesis1*, for all of its brokenness, is not utterly discordant. As we have seen, life at the level of *mimesis1* has all of the necessary ingredients for a narrative. It is a story waiting to be told. Yes, it is fragmented, episodic, and discordant, but it is in truth a "concordant discordance." Likewise, the narrative world of *mimesis2* is not utterly concordant. Everything is not neat and orderly. A good narrative has gaps, plot reversals, surprises, contingencies, and loose ends (this is also true, perhaps especially true, of biblical narratives, as we have seen in the discussion of Sternberg and Alter in the previous chapter). Yes, there is order, pattern, and concordance, but it is a "discordant concordance." When the hearer, who lives in the concordant discord of *mimesis1*, imaginatively enters the discordant concord of *mimesis2* through narrative, the result is not conformity. Instead the hearer "plays with the narrative constraints, brings about gaps, takes part in the combat between the [narrative and the antinarrative], and enjoys . . . the pleasure of the text."[44]

The hearer and the narrative cooperate in a creative and playful exchange. The narrative proposes a world, a configuration of the narrative potential in life, and the hearer enters into this world as an adventurer. But the journey does not stop here. In the jostling together of *mimesis1* and *mimesis2*, a new creation happens. The prefigured world of the hearer is gathered up into the configured world of the story, and on the other side of the transaction emerges that which did not exist before the encounter: the world of the hearer *refigured.* This refigured world is what Ricoeur calls *mimesis3.*

This understanding of narrative hermeneutics, applied to biblical preaching, means that preachers are to preach the biblical story, but not to stop at the level of the biblical text. The point is not merely to "teach the Bible," tell good stories that illustrate the biblical text, or even to enable the scripture to "come alive." The point is to call hearers to enter what Barth called "the strange new world within the Bible," or rather to call them to enter the world projected "in front of" the biblical text, and by entering into that world to become "new creation . . . [where] everything has become new" (2 Cor. 5:17).

From prefiguration, through configuration, to refiguration. This is how we should understand the power and the process of narrative preaching. Sermon stories don't just inspire and move people. Rather, they come into discordant and fragmented configurations of life and provide a temporary house of meaning and structure through which hearers potentially move to new configurations.

In his essay "Stories to Live By," Princeton sociologist Robert Wuthnow describes something of the same process as Ricoeur, when he describes how powerful stories and experiences become moral narratives that refigure our ethical lives. He tells about Jack Casey, a paramedic and ambulance driver. When Jack was a child, he had to have some dental surgery under general anesthetic, and he was terrified. One of the nurses said to him, "Don't worry, I'll be here right beside you, no matter what happens." And she was true to her word. When he woke up in recovery, she was right there.

Years later Jack was called to the scene of a highway accident. A man was pinned upside down in his pickup truck. The man was terrified and kept crying out that he was afraid of dying. Jack crawled inside the truck to reach him even though gasoline was dripping down on both of them. They were using power tools to cut the metal, so one spark could have meant a catastrophe. Jack nestled next to the man and said, "Look, don't worry, I'm right here with you, I'm not going anywhere." Almost exactly the same words he had heard so many years before from the nurse.

Later, the truck driver said to Jack, "'You were an idiot; you know that the thing could have exploded, and we'd have both been burned up!' And I told him I felt I just couldn't leave him."[45] From prefiguration (fear in the operating suite) through narrative configuration (the experience with nurse codified into a moral example) to refiguration (the almost unreflective action on the highway).

MIMETIC EXEGESIS

Ricoeur's description of the three levels of *mimesis* allows us to propose a kind of *mimetic* preaching, which can be based upon a particular style of biblical exegesis. In biblical exegesis for preaching, instead of searching for obvious analogies between the text and the contemporary context, or drawing "lessons" from the text, the preacher-exegete seeks to chart the arc of divine action in the text. Thus understood, the text is treated as a form of *mimetic2* action that exerts configuring power over the potentialities of the sermon, which consequently exerts *mimetic2* force upon the event of proclamation. In short, preaching enters into the world of the text seeking to discover the expression of the action of God there and then creatively imitates, describes, narrates, and proclaims that action in the sermon.

Here are two examples of the interpretation of biblical texts that show the difference that a mimetic understanding brings to exegesis for preaching:

1. **Exodus 22:26–27**—*If you take your neighbor's cloak in pawn, you shall restore it before the sun goes down; for it may be your neighbor's only clothing to use as cover; in what else shall that person sleep? And if your neighbor cries out to me, I will listen, for I am compassionate.* This piece of casuistic law seemingly offers little grist for the preaching mill. What is there to preach here? Taken without nuance, the text offers instructions to pawnbrokers; taken as a simple analogy, it at best gives clumsy ethical instruction for whatever situation in life the preacher decides is parallel to taking a coat in pawn from a destitute neighbor (maybe, "If your neighbor gets upside down in his mortgage and you buy his foreclosed house on the courthouse steps, you shall give it back before he is evicted"). But if, instead of trying to apply the text without interpretation or trying to wrangle out a strict analogy, we track the movement in the text, alert to the way the action of God arcs across human experience, another possibility emerges.

If you take your neighbor's cloak in pawn is directly addressed to the reader/hearer of this passage, and since we are in the world of the Torah, it is presumably God who is doing the speaking. This opening phrase places the reader/hearer into the middle of ordinary economic interaction, and in the position of power. "You" are the one who has exercised the power to "take" your neighbor's possession in pawn. Nothing unusual here. This is a customary economic transaction, but it is important to note that, as a character in *Saturday Night Live* might put it, "You are the broker, and your neighbor is the brokee."

. . . *you shall restore it before the sun goes down.* This kind of command normally completes the loop in casuistic legal expressions: *if* this is the case, *then* this is what the law requires, period. "*If* it is an election day, *then* no liquor shall be sold or consumed in the saloon." "If you take your neighbor's cloak in pawn . . ." is the case, and "you shall restore it before the sun goes down" is the law. Case closed.

But curiously, there is no closure. This text does not stop here, but instead moves on. If we continue to read the text, not only taking account of what it explicitly says but also imagining what it implies, we can see that this little bit of case law has set in motion a dialogue, or better yet an argument, between the "You" of the text and the God who speaks the law. Supplying the implied parts, here is how the debate goes:

God:	"If you take your neighbor's cloak in pawn, you shall restore it before the sun goes down."
You:	"Hey, wait a minute. That's not the way the world works! This is a pawn-broking deal, a quick loan. The cloak is the collateral. If I give it back before the loan is repaid, the whole concept of the transaction falls apart."
God:	"I know, but it may be your neighbor's only clothing to use as cover."
You:	"Exactly, that is why it works as collateral"
God:	"If you don't return the cloak at night, in what else shall your neighbor sleep?"
You:	"Not my problem."
God:	"Well, then, I am going to make it my problem. If your neighbor cries out to me, I will listen, for I am compassionate."

In the compress of a brief legal passage, then, we have been taken from the world of ordinary economic wheeling and dealing to the sanctuary, from the world of Wal-Mart to a theophany, from a world in which human power appears to proceed at its own pace and whim to a world where the God of compassion hears the cries of the needy and interrupts and disrupts human indifference.

2. Luke 17:26–30—*Just as it was in the days of Noah, so too it will be in the days of the Son of Man. They were eating and drinking, and marrying* *and being given in marriage, until the day Noah entered the ark, and the flood came and destroyed all of them. Likewise, just as it was in the days of Lot: they were eating and drinking, buying and selling, planting and building, but on the day that Lot left Sodom, it rained fire and sulfur from heaven and destroyed all of them—it will be like that on the day that the Son of Man is revealed.* Again, at first glance this does not appear to be the most fruitful of preaching texts. It seems to leave the preacher with a gloomy word, namely, that the last day, the "day that the Son of Man is revealed," is going to be a very bad day, and there are two Old Testament precedents—Noah and Lot—to back this up.

A closer reading of the text, however, with an open eye to the ways in which divine action is disclosed, cutting across the circumstances described in the passage, makes the picture more complex and richer:

Just as it was in the days of Noah, so too it will be in the days of the Son of Man. They were eating and drinking, and marrying and being given in marriage, until the day Noah entered the ark, and the flood came and destroyed all of them. The "days of the Son of Man" are compared to the "days of Noah" in the sense that people were engaged in various mundane activities ("eating and drinking, and marrying and being given in marriage"), oblivious to the impending catastrophe of the flood. Significantly, though, the English translation conceals an important feature of the Greek original, namely, that these activities are described by verbs in asyndeton, that is to say, without the usual conjunctions that would connect them (as in "I came, I saw, I conquered").[46] So instead of "eating and drinking, and marrying and being given in marriage," it is better rendered with the rhythmic, staccato "they were eating, drinking, marrying, affiancing." Moreover, these verbs in Greek are ἤσθιον, ἔπινον, ἐγάμουν, ἐγαμίζοντο (roughly pronounced "ess-thay-own, ep-eye-nown, egg-ah-mown, egg-ah-ma-zonto"). These verbs rhyme, and they create a distinctive rhetorical pattern. What were people in the days of Noah doing? Notice the rhythmic response: "Ess-thay-own, ep-eye-nown, egg-ah-mown, egg-ah-ma-zonto"—in short, "Yada, yada, yada." They were caught up in the normal, lulling rhythms of everyday life, quotidian existence as a two-martini lunch, and then the sudden and unexpected catastrophe destroyed it all.

Likewise, just as it was in the days of Lot: they were eating and drinking, buying and selling, planting and building, but on the day that Lot left Sodom, it rained fire and sulfur from heaven and destroyed all of them—it will be like that on the day that the Son of Man is revealed. This second example of "the days of Lot," while clearly a parallel to the previous "days of Noah," is no mere repetition, but rather, as is the case with parallelism in Hebrew poetry, it constitutes an extension and elaboration of the previous example. What were they doing in the days of Lot? They were "eating and drinking . . ." We have heard this list before. This is exactly what people were doing in the "days of Noah," and we know how this ends—with a world-shaking disaster. But unexpectedly the list expands, gathering in more and more arenas of life—"buying and selling, planting and building." This is the same rhythmic yada, yada, yada of the previous example, but the list of mundane activities has grown longer. We know from the "days of Noah" example that a divine catastrophe is coming at the end of the sentence, but *we do not know when the sentence will end.* Therefore, as the words rock back and forth in the seemingly ceaseless throbbing of everyday routine, we lean forward, alert to the coming divine shaking of the foundations that could come at any second. This passage has the effect of changing our body posture. While the culture flows along, caught up in the rhythms of seemingly immutable social habits and structures, the text urges us to lean forward into the future, toward a time when, by the action of God, the old world will pass way and the new creation will dawn.

To exegete biblical texts this way, attending to the ways that passages function in *mimesis2* fashion, configuring and then finally refiguring our religious imaginations, is to fulfill those words of Paul cited earlier, and to preach "with a demonstration of the Spirit and of power, so that . . . faith might rest not on human wisdom but on the power of God."

3

Nasty Suspicions, Conspiracy Theories, and the Return of Gnosticism

The contradictions and illiteracies of the New Testament have filled up many books by eminent scholars, and have never been explained by any Christian authority except in the feeblest terms of 'metaphor' and 'a Christ of faith.' This feebleness derives from the fact that until recently, Christians could simply burn or silence anybody who asked any inconvenient questions.

— Christopher Hitchens, *God Is Not Great*[1]

It ain't those parts of the Bible that I can't understand that bother me, it is the parts that I do understand.

—Mark Twain

More than three decades ago, theologian Edward Farley identified a "nasty suspicion" he saw worming its way down the halls of theological schools, namely, the chary notion that the church's language of faith is really only a matter of smoke and mirrors, that all of the church's talk about God is, when unmasked, merely empty lingo pointing to nothing. Farley named some of the questions lurking in the shadows of this nasty suspicion:

> Could it be that there are no realities at all behind the language of this historical faith? Could it be that the testimony, the storytelling, the liturgical expressions of this faith refer to entities that have only phenomenal status? Could it be that the mode of human existence which this historical religion calls faith involves no cognizing, no apprehendings, at all? Are Christian theologians like stockbrokers who distribute stock certificates on a nonexistent corporation? In this situation, the "reality" of the corporation, its size, type, power, and promise, turns out to be simply the stockbroker himself.[2]

Farley had in mind such thinkers as Lessing and Feuerbach and their impact on academic theology, but today this nasty suspicion that Christian leaders are like stockbrokers peddling junk bonds has made its way from the academy into church pews and is finding vigorous expression in congregations[3]—not everywhere, naturally, but especially among those the church desperately needs: the deepest thinking, best-read, most progressive, and most reflective churchgoers. There have always been doubters among the faithful, but what we are seeing now is not so much the usual kind of stubborn, "show me, I'm from Missouri" skepticism but more an informed, intelligent, probing set of challenges to the traditional formulations of the Christian faith on the part of many of the best and brightest lay folk.

Ironically, this new and nasty suspicion comes, in part, from something quite good: the sheer fact that many lay people are better informed than ever before about the historical and theological background of their faith. Take the Bible, for example. Armed with expertly annotated study Bibles and educated about the basics of textual criticism, thoughtful lay Christians today have an unprecedented critical understanding of scripture. They know that the biblical texts were not dropped down from heaven on golden tablets, pure and untouched, but are thoroughly edited, multilayered, and highly contested documents that are covered with the fingerprints of their many compilers and editors. Moreover, well-informed church people are now aware of a fact that might have shocked their parents, that there were a dozen or more "Gospels" (such as the *Gospel of Philip*, the *Gospel of Mary*, and the *Gospel of Thomas*) floating around in the first few centuries of the Christian movement. These Gospels, some with quite different visions of the faith from the New Testament Gospels, explode the myth of a dogmatically unified early church and are evidence that even very early on Christianity was so theologically and culturally diverse that some suggest that it could better be called "Christianities."

All of this newly acquired knowledge about Christian background on the part of lay folk is a welcome change, and it is placing a needed, if not always painless, demand on preachers and teachers. A faculty colleague of mine who is often invited as a guest lecturer to adult church school classes reported to me that he was astonished at the difference between what sometimes goes on "downstairs" in church school classrooms and what goes on "upstairs" in worship. Downstairs, people are full of sharp questions. They want to know about the historical Jesus, about discrepancies in the Gospels and whether they can be reconciled, about whether the apostle Paul extended or distorted the message of Jesus. They want to know how innocent suffering fits into ideas of the goodness of God, about other religions and their place in the economy of redemption, and about whether the idea of a God who acts in history is an outmoded myth. Downstairs, they have tough and urgent religious questions. Upstairs, however, they often get pabulum from the pulpit. They are all too frequently treated to sentimental and saccharine sermons that are devoid of intellectual fiber and that miss by a mile the probing concerns these bright lay people bring to their faith.

If we combine this deepened hunger for intellectual rigor and honesty with a more general spiritual restlessness in our culture, we can see why many serious lay people are worried and angry that the church does not address their urgent religious questions clearly or truthfully. Also, when they venture out on their own to explore these questions, what they discover about the origins of the Bible and the Christian faith seems to run counter to what they believe the church has taught them. Therefore, the nasty suspicion begins to develop inside the sanctuary. In most cases, this does not go as far as wondering if *all* talk of God is meaningless. Rather, it wonders if the *church's* talk is meaningless. The wary notion develops that the church's traditional and "official" way of describing God and the gospel has big holes in it. What is perhaps worse, there is the added suspicion that the church is participating in some kind of cover-up of the facts, keeping the lid on the real story of Christianity.

For instance, when a preacher in a sermon claims, without elaboration, "Jesus said, 'I am the bread of life,'" some in-the-know hearers go immediately on the alert. They are quite aware that there is a very good chance that Jesus did not say this at all, at least not in those exact words. They have learned that "I am the bread of life" in John's Gospel is one of several "I am" sayings and that all of them are most likely theological formulae *about* Jesus, which developed in the early church and were placed retroactively in Jesus' mouth. So why does the preacher not mention this? Does the preacher not know this? Does it make no difference whether the words are authentic to Jesus? Or worse, does the preacher actually want to conceal the fact that these words may be a doctrinal overlay from the later church? And, while we're asking, what is the real story on all those other Gospels, the ones that lost out to Matthew, Mark, Luke, and John? Were they less trustworthy, or did they instead get suppressed because they contained views that threatened the ecclesiastical establishment? Biblical scholar Bart Erhman speaks for many in the church today when he says, "Someone decided that four of these early Gospels, and no others, should be accepted as part of the canon—the collection of sacred books of Scripture. But how did they make their decisions? When? How can we be sure they were right? And whatever happened to the other books?"[4]

For many of the best educated, most inquisitive church folk, the hunch is growing that behind the church's whole way of talking about things—behind the biblical stories of the Red Sea parting and of Jesus walking on the water, behind the claims that Jesus is the divine Son of God and that the risen Christ appeared in bodily form to his followers on Easter—is another, hidden story, a story that is somehow more plausible, more historically accurate, more down to earth, and finally more believable. Moreover, the suspicion grows that the church, to protect its power and creed, has been less than forthcoming about the true history, peddling instead a party line, a mythical, magical, biased, and outdated version of things—"like stockbrokers," as Farley said, "who distribute stock certificates on a nonexistent corporation."

CONSPIRACY THEORIES AND SPIRITUAL QUESTS

There are two broad expressions of the nasty suspicion growing in and about the church. The first and more extreme, located especially in the popular religious imagination, takes the form of fascination with more or less outright conspiracy theories. The church does not speak candidly, it is alleged, because it is engaging in sinister damage control over embarrassing facts. A radio talk show host in Atlanta, after spending several minutes taking way too seriously the twisted plots and fanciful schemes of Dan Brown's blockbuster novel *The Da Vinci Code*, said, "And another thing. I'd like to find out what really happened at this . . . what did they call it? . . . the Council of Nicaea. I understand that all of the bishops in the church met behind closed doors and voted that Jesus was God! And the vote was very close!" One imagines scores of incognito bishops slipping by night into a remote Bithynian hideaway, locking the doors, and hatching a plot to improve their pension plans by turning Christianity from the flagging social reform movement of a failed backwater prophet into a "major world religion" by voting him into divine status.

Or consider the smugly confident prose of this announcement issued by cable television's Discovery Channel:

New scientific evidence, including DNA analysis conducted at one of the world's foremost molecular genetics laboratories, as well as studies by leading scholars, suggests a 2,000-year-old Jerusalem tomb could have once held the remains of Jesus of Nazareth and his family. The findings also suggest that Jesus and Mary Magdalene might have produced a son named Judah.[5]

We picture a team of brainy scientists in their crisp white lab coats working tirelessly in "one of the world's foremost molecular genetics laboratories" (where? Harvard? Oxford? Dr. No's secret laboratory in the Caribbean?) swirling beakers of liquid solvent containing traces of DNA from Galilee's most talked about couple, Jesus and Mary Magdalene, and carefully entering data into a computer program.

Never mind that the bishops at the Council of Nicaea did not for a minute question or debate the truthfulness of Jesus' divinity but were instead concerned, in the face of the Arian controversy, with precisely how to define the relationship of the divine and the human in Christ. Never mind that most reliable biblical and archaeological specialists find that the claim that the tomb excavated in Jerusalem in 1980 contains the remains of the biblical Jesus and Mary Magdalene should be placed somewhere on a scale between extremely speculative and outright hokum, and the notion that Jesus and Mary had a child together is a tantalizing piece of tabloid gossip with not a shred of persuasive evidence to support it. Such unconventional accounts nevertheless have deep appeal to a popular religious imagination ever ready to say, "I knew it! Now the real story comes out!"

In a milder and more academic way, the Jesus Seminar, the group of biblical scholars who met over a number of years to sift the historically authentic sayings of Jesus in the Gospels from the "inauthentic" ones, claimed to have ferreted out a churchly conspiracy of their own. Seminar founder Robert Funk, in a somewhat Napoleonesque address to the group's inaugural assembly, claimed that the work of the Jesus Seminar would "spell liberty for . . . millions."[6] Funk went on to explain that these millions were being held captive to the obstructionist censorship of truthful information by their own church leaders and their media coconspirators:

> Make no mistake: there is widespread and passionate interest in this issue, even among those uninitiated in the higher mysteries of gospel scholarship. The religious establishment has not allowed the intelligence of high scholarship to pass through pastors and priests to a hungry laity, and the radio and TV counterparts of educated clergy have traded in platitudes and pieties and played on the ignorance of the uninformed. A rude and rancorous awakening lies ahead.[7]

What are we to imagine here? That in the glass and steel denominational headquarters of—take your pick: the Lutherans, the Methodists, the Presbyterians—powerful church executives hold secret meetings to devise strategies to keep "the intelligence of high scholarship" from passing into the undeserving hands of "a hungry laity"? In a way, it's flattering to "the religious establishment" to think that they would have that kind of power and skill to carry off such an elaborate conspiracy, and to keep the media on a leash while they do it. Most branches of "the religious establishment" have trouble shipping Sunday school curriculum materials accurately. It boggles the mind to contemplate that they could dam up the entire flow of knowledge between the academy and the churches.

Conspiracy theories may burn wildly, but they do so because they are fueled on the stubble of mistrust. Recently, *National Geographic* made a cause célèbre over the surfacing of the long-lost *Gospel of Judas*, with its "shocking secret" that Judas Iscariot was, in truth, the hero of the Jesus story and not its villain. This second-century document turns the Gospel accounts on their heads. Judas is presented not as Jesus' betrayer, but as the most favored of Jesus' disciples, the one follower who alone understood that Jesus desired to be handed over to the authorities. In a newspaper interview, Donald Senior, president of Chicago's Catholic Theological Union and professor of New Testament, put the discovery in proper perspective. Aware that the *Gospel of Judas* was one of a number of later gnostic Gospels whose teachings were already well known, Professor Senior assured the reporter that the surfacing of this new text conveyed no dramatically new information and posed no immediate threat to traditional understandings of Christianity. The reporter summarized Senior's view: "[T]he Gnostic Gospels could undermine Christianity only if many Christians were to adopt the kind of conspiracy thinking that undergirds *The Da Vinci Code*: that an "orthodox elite" of early church authorities suppressed the free-thinking, spiritual Gnostics 'for the sake of uniformity and conformity.'" Then, perhaps suddenly remembering that many Christians and others in fact *do* put stock in such conspiracies, Senior quipped, "I'm just glad it wasn't found in a bank vault in the Vatican."[8]

Preachers today are speaking to congregations who have watched the Discovery Channel and read *USA Today* and have been exposed to every overheated media report of archaeological finds that will allegedly destroy Christianity. Addressing notions of conspiracy may be painstaking, but with time, good sense, and a large dose of the facts, it can be done. It is not, perhaps, the most glorious task of the pulpit, but when a deep suspicion arises in the congregation over some media flap, it may be a necessary task. When Paul was on trial before King Festus for his missionary activities, one of the arguments he felt necessary to make in his defense was that the gospel does not involve secrecy or cover-ups but happens out in plain view. "Indeed the king knows about these things," said Paul, "and to him I speak freely; for I am certain that none of these things has escaped his notice, for this was not done in a corner" (Acts 26:26).

There is, however, a second expression of the nasty suspicion loose in the community of faith. This expression needs to be taken much more seriously by preachers, because it is not found on talk radio or on the shelves of the airport bookshop; it is found in the pews. It is right there among the church's "best and brightest": committed, intelligent, and well-read lay folk who earnestly desire to hold onto their Christian faith and their church commitments but who also either do not entirely trust what their church has taught them or who have simply discovered, through reading and intelligent probing, that Christian history is more complex, contentious, and varied than they had realized. They experience a tension between what they read and think, on the one hand, and what they believe they hear from their churches, on the other. For the most part, this tension causes them not to flee the church or the faith outright, but it sets them on an uncharted quest for an alternative form of Christian spirituality. They seek a living faith that steps lightly over the rubble of traditionalism, dogmatism, and institutionally bound forms of religion. They want a nonconventional engagement with the holy, a spirituality that seems more savvy, more honest, less hidebound, more able to face the historical facts, freer, and more uplifting that the kind of Christianity traditionally advocated by the church. They want to read the Bible intelligently, worship with eyes wide open, ask the difficult questions, have a faith that makes sense, and participate fully in the life of the Christian community without checking their minds at the door.

An admirable quest? Yes, of course, and it is a sad commentary that these lay folk have, in too many instances, not found their minds engaged, their imaginations nourished, and their souls invigorated by the preaching and teaching of their pastors. In fact, those who hunger for this new and more authentic form of spirituality find refreshment from many springs—meditation, nature, spiritual exercises—but many have discovered a group of conversation partners outside of their local churches: theologians, biblical scholars, and religious philosophers whose works seem to speak more clearly and more directly—and in their view, more honestly—to their needs, writers like John Shelby

Spong, Elaine Pagels, Matthew Fox, Bart D. Ehrman, Karen Armstrong, and Marcus Borg.

In *The Heart of Christianity,* a book specifically addressed to those who want to find a passionate Christianity that does not require "a sacrifice of the intellect,"[9] Borg indicates that this quest has created a division between the earnest questers and more traditional Christians:

> Christians in North America today are deeply divided about the heart of Christianity. We live in a time of major conflict in the church. Millions of Christians are embracing an emerging way of seeing Christianity's heart. Millions of other Christians continue to embrace an earlier version of Christianity, often insistently defending it as "traditional" Christianity and as the only legitimate way of being Christian.[10]

Spong, the retired bishop of the Episcopal Diocese of Newark, New Jersey, is more acerbic. He presents the division not only as one between traditional "churchy" Christian pew-sitters, on the one hand, and those who seek the more freeing "God experience in Jesus," on the other, but especially as a battle between determined, honest, intellectually curious lay folk and their fearful, controlling, self-protective pastors:

> Critical biblical scholarship, having now passed through several generations, forms the frame of reference in which the Christian academy works, dramatically separating the Bible from the assumptions held by the average pew-sitters in our various churches. Yet clergy, trained for the most part in the academy, seem to join a conspiracy of silence to suppress this knowledge when they become pastors, fearful that if that average pew-sitter learned the content of the real debate, his or her faith would be destroyed—and with it, more importantly, his or her support for institutional Christianity.[11]

Spong here imagines that most clergy take the same attitude toward critical biblical scholarship that a British dowager of the nineteenth century took toward Darwin. When told of Darwin's theory of evolution, she exclaimed, "Oh my, I hope it isn't true! But if it is, I hope it won't become widely known."

Spong is cynical and mistaken, however, about the motives of the clergy. The vast majority of well-trained pastors are eager for their congregations to go on a quest for knowledge, to inhale great gulps of critical biblical scholarship, historical background, and theological content. In fact, hundreds of thousands of lay Christians in the United States have, with the encouragement of their pastors, engaged in intensive, critically informed programs of Bible study such as *Kerygma* and *Disciple Bible Study*. The problem for most clergy is usually not motive, but know-how. Many clergy yearn for their parishioners to be well informed, deeply committed disciples, but they simply do not know how to help them. They do not know how, in their preaching and teaching, to convey the life-giving, freeing, passionate white-water adventure that is to be found in the scriptures, creeds, traditions, theological explorations, and practices of the Christian community. So they leave these questing parishioners to follow their own noses. Moreover, ironically, a good many mainline clergy are themselves in the same position as these seeking laypeople. Clergy swim in the same cultural stream as everyone else, and many clergy too are unsure of the trustworthiness of the church's language about God, perplexed about what to make of the scriptures and the theological traditions of the church, and they hardly know where to turn for help.

The result, to focus on preaching, is that sermons often step around the intellectual and theological challenges of the faith in favor of a safer, less conflicted, and already digested word. Sermons speak words of pastoral comfort, or they call for ethical engagement on the issues of the day, but they do not much wrestle with the intellectual challenges that stand in the way of many believers. It is easy to preach "God loves you unconditionally, even in your deepest distress" or "God's people are called to stand for peace and justice," without ever going behind those slogans to engage the tough theological issues involved in making such claims. As a consequence, deprived of the intellectual struggle and a vital sense of the gospel, the church's preached faith can seem pale, out of touch, lifeless. The creeds can seem like rote, take-it-or-leave-it dogmatic moments in the liturgy, rather than expressions of hard-won, blood-stained wisdom wrung from of centuries of wrestling with the meaning of God and human experience. The church's passion for the life-giving treasure it has been given in the gospel can come across as defensive, authoritarian, and self-protective. And when the inevitable bungle or scandal or power play mars its life, the church can easily appear to be just another cumbersome, oppressive, and Machiavellian institution getting in the way of the free wind of the Spirit.

By contrast, Borg, Pagels, Spong, Armstrong, Ehrman, and company are superb and confident communicators, apparently open-mindedly facing the hard questions and the big problems, and quietly many inquisitive Christians are finding themselves challenged, informed, and fed by them. They present complex religious concepts in clear, straight-forward fashion with persuasive and seemingly intellectually cogent arguments. As one Christian lawyer, who had just finished reading Pagels's quite personal struggle with creedal Christianity in her book *Beyond Belief*,[12] said to his pastor, "Hey, can you explain Elaine Pagels to me? I hope you can, because she's making a hell of a lot more sense to me than your sermons are!"

THE RETURN OF THE GNOSTIC IMPULSE

We need now to ask, however, what precisely is this new and "more authentic" form of spirituality taking shape among seekers in the church? What is it that is making "a hell of a lot more sense" to some parishioners than our sermons? What kind of Christian expression do Borg, Pagels, Spong, and the others help to shape among these searching folk, lay and clergy? If Borg is right that there are indeed "millions of Christians . . . embracing an emerging way of seeing Christianity's heart," what is this emerging way? Of course, there is no one name to give it. There are too many people responding out of too many different motives in too many diverse contexts to catch up this spiritual restless-ness in a single stitch. But Borg is right. A large number of people are heading out on spiritual pilgrimages down more or less similar paths, concerned about a host of the same issues, and in conversation with many of the same writers, and this has the feel of a religious and cultural movement within the church. The iceberg out there in the dark sea has many jagged edges, but we can make out its basic shape nevertheless.

I am convinced that a major element in this movement toward an alternative form of spirituality is the return of a gnostic impulse in Chris-tianity. Borg, Spong, Pagels, and the others did not invent this renewed gnostic impulse, and to some degree they don't even advocate for it, but they do feed it. I use this phrase "gnostic impulse" carefully and advis-edly. First, by employing the word "gnostic" I am making a historical analogy. I want to suggest that some aspects of today's search for an alter-native spirituality are similar to characteristics found in one of the earli-est theological challenges faced by the church: the Christian gnosticism that developed over the first three centuries of the church's life.[13]

Christian gnosticism was a highly variegated theological movement that focused on salvation by illumination (via special knowledge, *gnōsis*). It interpreted the scriptures and the story of Jesus in ways quite different from what came to be accepted as orthodox Christianity. "Gnosticism," states New Testament scholar Raymond Brown, "is so diverse it almost defies definition. In general, its Christian proponents claimed special knowledge—about the divine status of human beings— that had been obscured in the Old Testament but was revealed by the elect by Jesus, who was thus regarded as an illuminator rather than a dying savior."[14] Second-century gnosticism in its pure form is a thing of the past, but echoes of it reverberate in the new spirituality.

Also, I use the terms "gnostic impulse" and "gnosticism" (lowercase) rather than "Gnosticism" to make it clear that I am talking about a dynamic way of envisioning the religious life and not a clearly identifiable historical movement. There is no unbroken historical line that can be neatly drawn from those called gnostics in the early Christian era to the spiritual seekers who hunger today for an alternative spirituality. Gnosticism is not like Lutheranism or even Pentecostalism in that current adherents of those movements can point back to Wittenberg or the Azusa Street revival and trace their theological lineage forward. Gnosticism has no such institutional memory, no authoritative canon of scriptures, no accepted history of doctrinal development, no structures by which authority is maintained and passed on. Rather the "gnostic impulse" is a counterforce, a reaction that erupts here and there in church history in response to what is seen as the barrenness and oppressiveness of what the church is teaching.[15]

The church has experienced the rise of the gnostic impulse many times, but each time it wears a different face. As Pagels suggests, "The concerns of gnostic Christians survived only as a suppressed current, like a river driven underground. Such currents surfaced throughout the Middle Ages in various forms of heresy; then with the Reformation, Christian tradition again took on new and diverse forms."[16] What Pagels calls the "suppressed current" of gnosticism has again bubbled to the surface and is sloshing around in Christian congregations, especially among educated parishioners.

But who are these new gnostics? What is the contemporary gnostic impulse? Why should pastors and preachers be concerned about all of this? Before we start looking under the bushes for gnostics in our midst, we need to observe a few cautions. First, we can claim too much for the term "gnostic." To use "gnostic" in the dynamic way we are using it runs the risk of allowing it to spill over the banks and flood the whole land. Some in fact argue that everything about Western culture today is basically gnostic. Post-Enlightenment civilization is so thoroughly marked by an insistence on individual autonomy, a search for personal freedom, a quest to find spiritual wisdom within, and a resistance to external structures of authority that it is easy to see the whole apple as "gnostic" to the core. If this is true, then "gnostic" is simply an accusing label we paste on those aspects of modern life we happen not to like. Historian of religion Ioan Culianu once mocked the all-embracing uses of "gnostic" that he found abounding in scholarship:

> Not only Gnosis was gnostic, but the catholic authors were gnostic, the neoplatonic too, Reformation was gnostic, Communism was gnostic, Nazism was gnostic, liberalism, existentialism and psycho-analysis were gnostic too, modern biology was gnostic, Blake, Yeats, Kafka, Rilke, Proust, Joyce, Musil, Hesse and Thomas Mann were gnostic. From the very authoritative interpreters of Gnosis, I learned further that science is gnostic and superstition is gnostic; power, counter-power, and lack of power are gnostic; left is gnostic and right is gnostic; Hegel is gnostic and Marx is gnostic; Freud is gnostic and Jung is gnostic; all things and their opposites are equally gnostic.[17]

Second, we should know that the term "gnostic" is controversial, and can be a fighting word. The whole vocabulary of gnosticism has become contested territory. Some say that "gnosticism" is a hopelessly unstable term and should be avoided, because it implies some coherent and unified movement that never actually existed.[18] True, the picture we have of gnosticism since the discovery of the collection of gnostic writings at Nag Hammadi in 1945 is much more varied and complex, that is to say fuzzier, than it appeared when we knew about gnosticism only second-hand, via the sharp-tongued attacks on it in the writings of the church fathers. Other scholars make the even stronger charge that the term "gnosticism" is corrupt and ideologically loaded from the beginning. It was, after all, the orthodox opponents of the gnostics who first slapped that label on them. The name "gnostics" (*gnōstikoi*, implying those who think they know something) started out, like "Methodists" and "Impressionists," as a sneer before it became a description. Some others even catch a whiff of heresy hunting in the term. To call someone "gnostic," they say, is a sword wielded by conservative reactionaries on the warpath against liberals. As Bryan K. Sholl puts it:

> For theologians decrying the attenuation of orthodox theology, this thesis [that Gnosticism has returned in modern garb] applies primarily to nineteenth-and twentieth-century liberal theology, and is

meant to cast suspicion on the host of political, literary and religious movements known as secular modernity. It is a term of opprobrium often used as a conversation stopper, and when used maliciously, as an implication of heretical intent.[19]

I want to be clear: by using the phrase "gnostic impulse" I am not on a heresy hunt. I do not think for a second that the seekers in the church who are on a quest for a new kind of spirituality are anything close to "heretics," whatever that might mean in today's context. In fact, I think they are yearning for what all Christians should desire: an informed, intelligent faith that gives powerful meaning to persons and that can make sense of itself in the world. I also believe that part of what set them off on their quest in the first place is a set of failures by the church and its pulpit. We often have been silent when we should have spoken, garrulous when we should have listened, muddled when we should have been clear, and controlling when we should have been life giving.

On the other hand, something crucial is at stake here. Gnosticism today leads people, as it always has, into a theological, spiritual, and ethical cul-de-sac. It settles for a distorted version of the gospel, one that misses the full meaning, power, hope, and joy of the real thing. Many of these questers are, to borrow Van Harvey's memorable phrase, "most distrustful of just those answers [they] would most like to believe,"[20] and it is the duty and the delight of the preacher to present the gospel clearly and compellingly in the light of the real concerns and questions these seekers bring.

At the deepest level the gospel is not threatened, and it is not our role to defend and protect the gospel. The gospel is the truth; it can take care of itself. But when we remember that the gospel is not just a set of truth claims but a way of being in the world, then at the pastoral level the gospel is imperiled every day, and it is indeed the role of the church's leaders, preachers, teachers, and pastors to enable people to hear the good news rightly and to trust it and live it out. For example, when a young couple gets up in the morning only to discover to their horror that their newborn has died in the night, they have more than simply grief and profound sorrow. They have theological questions. Where was God in this? What kind of God would allow this? What hope is there for them and for their baby? To set them adrift to seek their own answers to these aching and important questions would be pastorally irresponsible. What if they decide that God was punishing them for their sins by taking their child's life? What if they decide that earthly life is only misery and captivity and that it was a good thing that their child died and was spared having to go through this vale of tears? A good pastor would not leave these misconceptions unchallenged; what they believe about God and life matters profoundly.

Just so, engaging the new gnosticism in the church is a signal pastoral and homiletical responsibility. In the New Testament, we already see this pastoral effort to take on gnostic thought (in Paul and the Gospel of John in particular), and we find a sustained critique of gnosticism in Ignatius, Justin Martyr, Irenaeus, Tertullian, Hippolytus, Origen, and many others among the earliest Christian theologians.[21]

ONE STORY, TWO VERSIONS

The way we view the gnostic impulse in the church today depends, in part, on how we tell this story of the early gnostics, who they were, and what happened to them. There are basically two ways to narrate it. The first story line is that the early church made a terrible mistake in thinking of the gnostics as a threat to the gospel, rather than recognizing them as the sign of a welcome theological diversity. In the early years of the Christian movement, as this story goes, the question of how to ascribe meaning to the event of Jesus was completely up for grabs. There were some Christians who interpreted the Jesus event and the Christian faith in the ways that have come to be accepted as catholic and apostolic Christianity, but there were plenty of other Christians, including those we now call "gnostics," who had different takes on such matters as the understanding of God, the identity of Jesus, the character of faith, the role of women in the community, the nature of the resurrection, and so on. These other Christians, goes the story, had views that were just as worthy, just as rich, as the first group, but their problem was disorganization. They loved the truth, but, alas, they couldn't organize a precinct. But the first group, with politically savvy leaders like Bishop Irenaeus, maneuvered themselves into positions of power and systematically stamped out their opponents' views. In short, the church could have had beautiful theological diversity and a richness of spiritual options, but it chose instead uniformity, authoritarian control, and domination.

This is essentially the story that Pagels tells in *The Gnostic Gospels*. "To the impoverishment of the Christian tradition," she writes, "gnosticism, which offered alternatives to what became the main thrust of Christian orthodoxy, was forced outside."[22] Seen this way, the early battles against gnosticism were actually more political than pastoral, "gnostic" was simply a demonizing label applied to people who dared to disagree with the bishops, and the attempts to counter gnosticism were little more than power plays on the part of the establishment. "Only by suppressing gnosticism," argues Pagels, "did orthodox leaders establish that system of organization which united all believers into a single institutional structure."[23]

Bart Ehrman agrees. A strong group of early Christians battled a weaker group over what constitutes "correct" Christianity, he claims, and when the strong party won the battle, they added a note of treachery. "And then," Ehrman states, "this victorious party rewrote the history of the controversy, making it appear that there had not been much of a conflict at all, claiming that its own views . . . had always been 'orthodox.'"[24]

Naturally, this first story of what happened has the side effect of making the gnostics into romantic heroes for a certain swath of left-leaning Christians who themselves feel like underdogs and victims in the truth versus power game. Historian Kathleen McVey, reviewing Pagels's book, comments,

> Elaine Pagels's *Gnostic Gospels* is a book calculated to appeal to the liberal intellectual Christian who feels personally religious but who dislikes "institutional religion." Pagels has presented us with an appealing portrayal of the gnostic Christians as a beleaguered minority of creative persons deprived of their rightful historical role by a well-organized but ignorant lot of literalists.[25]

One contemporary fan of the gnostics is even more rhapsodic abut their virtues:

> [The Gnostics] focused on the individual rather than the group. They were liberals rather than holy tories; the Quakers and Anabaptists of their day, not the Romans or High Anglicans. They were hippies, not corporate executives; spiritual people rather than attendees at divine services; they saw salvation in enlightenment, not ecclesiastical sanction; they were seekers after blessedness, not recipients of blessing; a priesthood of believers rather than believers in the priesthood. They were idealists, not church-builders; people who would cheer for Ivan Karamazov, not for the Grand Inquisitor.[26]

If we accept this first version of the story, what open-minded, caring Christian wouldn't want to take up the cause of the gnostics, or at least make room for them? The gnostics bring diversity and a hunger for freedom. These are people of the heart rather than people of the cumbersome institution. Why crush them under the heavy millstone of orthodoxy? Why even think about, much less scrutinize, the contemporary gnostic impulse? We all have our versions of spirituality. Let a thousand flowers bloom.

There is, however, another way to tell the story, a way less infected with Nietzschean preoccupations with power and, I am persuaded, more accurate. Yes, the theological positions of the earliest church were in flux. Yes, there is a political dimension to the account of how the church got from amazement of Easter to the creedal affirmations of the Council of Nicaea. But the main theme in this second telling of the story is not one of naked political power plays and strong-arm bishops muscling minority viewpoints out of the way and concocting revisionist history, but one of Christians testing and sifting ideas over time. It is a narrative of the church attempting to describe the meaning of the Jesus event over against its memories and experiences and in the light of Jesus Christ sensed as a living presence in its worship and mission. Such testing and shifting was not done, of course, in the polite civility of a debate club, but in the rough and tumble of the church's life. The process was sometimes jagged, often adversarial, and, like all other human processes, never free from blemish, but it was aimed at listening to the Spirit and shaping the life of the church around Christ. Paul, for example, moves aggressively, perhaps even sarcastically, in challenging the Corinthians' thin views of the resurrection ("Now if Christ is proclaimed as raised from the dead, how can some of you say there is no resurrection of the dead?" [1 Cor. 15:12]), but this is no church politician suppressing dissent. This is a pastor pleading for the lives and souls of his congregation.[27]

According to this telling of the story, certain ways of seeing the faith—like gnosticism—and certain documents that had a short burst of popularity among early Christians—like the *Gospel of Mary*—moved to the periphery and sank out of sight, not because their advocates were politically naive and victims of domination, but mainly because these ideas and documents finally proved intellectually, theologically, and ethically inadequate. They did not, in the long run, prove able to shape healthy Christian faith. "The crystallization of what came to be known as orthodoxy," notes Nock, "was a gradual process, a progressive elimination of ideas which proved unacceptable."[28]

If two thousand years from now someone digging under a horse barn in Nag Hammadi, Texas, should unearth a clay jar holding a moldy copy of the long-forgotten *Your Best Life Now* by Joel Osteen, forty-first-century Christians will have two choices. They could exclaim, "How wonderful to have in our hands the actual text of this 'lost Christianity'! We had previously known of it only through the attacks of its twenty-first-century detractors, who distorted and demonized it, but now we can hear the voice of the prosperity gospel in its own right, and our range of alternative spiritualities is enriched." Or they could read the book and realize why it fell into oblivion. Raymond Brown, using more caustic language than I would, nevertheless is on target when he refers to the writings of the early gnostics and says that just reading them could leave one convinced that "crusty old Irenaeus was right, after all, to regard the gnostics as the crazies of the second century."[29]

The view of early Christian theologians and leaders as power politicians also badly misses the point. Yes, people are people and politics is involved in even the best aspects of church life, but the deepest reason the early church leaders fought so hard against gnosticism is not because they were grabbing power. It was rather because they genuinely believed that true life was to be found in allegiance to the God who created heaven and earth and to the Christ who, in the swirl of human history, put his body on the cross and who was raised by God, in an astonishing Easter victory, bodily from the dead, and not in a commitment to a disembodied, self-probing, ahistorical, world-denying, spiritual gnosis. These early theologians were not boxing at shadows. As Lee states, "It would seem either that the gnostics posed a grave threat to Christianity or else that the Fathers were suffering from a pathological obsession, for this question seems to have absorbed so much of their considerable talents and energies."[30]

Moreover, to see the struggles against gnosticism in the early church as mainly political ignores the historical context. These early bishops were not church fat cats, living in palaces and gliding to confabs in limos. As Luke Johnson has pointed out, "Irenaeus became bishop of Lyons because his predecessor was martyred. Being Christian was still a dangerous occupation."[31] N. T. Wright, after reminding his readers of the terrible persecutions of Christians that took place in second-century Vienne and Lyons, scoffs at the notion that the fight against gnosticism was really only a matter of empire building:

Nothing could be further from the truth. The people who were being burned at the stake, fried on hot irons, thrown to the wild beasts, pulled apart on the rack, and the other delights [of the martyrs of Vienne and Lyons]—these people did not imagine themselves to be on the way to a great political victory of "orthodoxy" over "heresy." They were not, as is often suggested, settling down and making comfortable compromises with the status quo. . . . They were following their crucified Lord. If what you want to do is advance a program for ecclesial structure and control . . . it hardly seems sensible to embrace and teach a message which is likely to get you and the other key leaders tortured and killed.[32]

CONTEMPORARY GNOSTICISM: FOUR THEMES

So with both urgency and caution, let us return to the question of the shape of the gnostic impulse in the church today. Drawing upon the historical analogy with earlier forms, we can identify four broad themes in contemporary gnosticism:[33]

1. Humanity is "saved" by gnosis, by knowledge. Perhaps the most characteristic marker of the gnostic impulse is the belief that human beings, given the proper knowledge, given illumination, can learn their way to wholeness. The gnostic impulse does not imagine humanity captive to sin and needing divine rescue. In fact, the idea of a sinful humanity is minimized, even repudiated. In traditional Christian thought, knowing what is good, even willing what is good, does not necessarily entail doing what is good. "I do not do the good I want, but the evil I do not want is what I do," said Paul (Rom. 7:19). In the gnostic impulse, however, the human problem is not sin but ignorance, and the ethical implication is that people, when they are fully enlightened, will choose the good.

2. An antipathy toward incarnation and embodiment. Almost every human being is perplexed by the presence of evil, suffering, and injustice in the world and wonders how it is possible for a good God to have created such a pain-filled and broken world. The response of the ancient gnostics was that the "real" God had nothing to do with the creation of this corrupt world. They had a good cop/bad cop understanding of divinity; there were two gods, the "good" god above all time and circumstance and the "bad" or lower god, who created this mess.

As Birger Pearson states, "In terms of theology, the Gnostics split the transcendent God of the Bible into two: a super-transcendent supreme God who is utterly alien to the world, and a lower deity who is responsible for creating and governing the world in which we live."[34] The goal of enlightenment was for the human spirit to escape the material world and the body and to achieve reunion with the transcendent God.

While very few today would hold to a "good spiritual god" versus a "bad creator god" theology, the effects of this dualism linger. Contemporary gnostics are allergic to flesh and embodiment, to history and structure. Ross Douthat, an editor at the *Atlantic Monthly*, once described Bart Ehrman as "the ex-fundamentalist who abandoned Christianity once it became clear to him that there might have been actual human beings involved in the composition of its sacred texts."[35] A wry quip, but one that nonetheless hits the bull's-eye about gnosticism. Traditional Christianity, while fully realistic about human sinfulness, nevertheless sees human flesh and history as a place that God has chosen to dwell, a place thus made sacred. But for gnostics, human rituals, structures, and institutions are at best unfortunate and accidental necessities, and at worst contaminants. All that smacks of the earthly and time-bound is seen as inferior to the timeless and eternal. Spiritual experiences are good; creeds are embodied encrustations and are to be avoided. Heartfelt moments of illumination are good; messy religious institutions are inevitably corrupt.

Writing in the *New York Times*, columnist David Brooks noted that many Christians have been busily responding to the recent spate of popular bestselling books challenging the existence of God. But defending God's existence, claimed Brooks, is the easy part. "The real challenge," he went on to say, "is going to come from people who feel the existence of the sacred, but who think that particular religions are just cultural artifacts built on top of universal human traits." Religions, churches, confessions, scriptures, doctrines—all fleshly, human-made things. The gnostic impulse finds it hard to swallow the gospel claim that the Word became flesh and lived among us. Rather, for the gnostics, the Word is always becoming spirit and floating above us. The gnostic impulse is "spiritual but not religious."

From the very beginning, gnostics have been particularly bothered by the notion of the resurrection of the body, including, of course, the claim that Jesus was raised in bodily form. In the world of Greek thought in which gnosticism developed, the body was considered to be a "bag of dung," and true religion was a means to get free from its corrupting effects. Gnostics, therefore, prefer to speak of the immortality of the soul, of souls being reunited with God, of a purer spiritual experience that does not entail dragging along the embarrassment of a body. As Bart Ehrman rightly observes,

> According to most gnostics, this material world is *not* our home. We are trapped here, in these bodies of flesh, and we need to learn how to escape. . . . Since the point is to allow the soul to leave this world behind and to enter into "that great and holy generation"—that is, the divine realm that transcends this world—a resurrection of the body is the very last thing that Jesus, or any of his true followers, would want.[36]

So what do the new gnostics do with the New Testament claims of resurrection? Here is how Spong describes what "really happened" in the "Easter moment":

> One night in the early fall, Simon and his mates had a particularly good catch. They were happy as they dragged the fish ashore. They built a fire, placed some of their catch on the grill, brought out the bread from the boat, and prepared to feast. As was his custom, Simon took the bread, said the ceremonial blessing, broke and distributed it. In his blessing, he likened the bread to Jesus' broken body. Both, he said, were meant to give life.
> Then it happened. A light went on in Simon's head. It was as if the heavens opened and so did Simon's eyes, and Simon stared into the realm of God. There he saw Jesus as part of God's being and God's meaning. It was not delusional. Death could not destroy the one who made God known. "Death cannot contain him. I have seen the Lord!" was Simon's ecstatic exclamation. Then Simon opened the eyes of the others to what he saw. Each of them grasped this vision, experienced Jesus alive, and were themselves resurrected. That was Easter. It was both objective and subjective, but above all it was real.[37]

Notice that here the resurrection is not embodied. There is no risen Christ asking for fish and saying things like, "Touch me and see; for a ghost does not have flesh and bones as you see I have" (Luke 24:39). This resurrection is something that happens "in Simon's head." It's clean; it's pure; it's spiritual; it's illumination.

It is also gnosticism.

3. A focus on the spiritual inner self, the "divine spark" within. In the gnostic impulse, the quest for God always involves a turn inward.

As Bloom describes gnostic religion, "It is a knowing, by and of an uncreated self, or self-within-the-self, and the knowledge leads to freedom . . . from nature, time, history, community, other selves."[38] The new gnostic's favorite verse of scripture (taken out of context) is: "Neither shall they say, Lo here! or, Lo there! for, behold, the kingdom of God is within you" (Luke 17:21 KJV). Focused on the inward kingdom of God, the gnostic impulse runs perilously close to conflating the divine and the human, seeing human beings as pieces of the divine trapped in fleshly bodies. Elaine Pagels quotes Monoimus, a gnostic teacher, who advises his disciples to quit looking for God "out there" and to take up instead the inward quest:

> Abandon the search for God and the creation and other matters of a similar sort. . . . Learn who it is within you who makes everything his own and says, "My God, my mind, my thought, my soul, my body." Learn the sources of sorrow, joy, love, hate . . . if you carefully investigate these matters you will find him *in yourself*."[39]

In Jim Harrison's novel *True North*, David Burkett, the young scion of a Michigan timber family, is off on a religious and personal quest. Converted and baptized at a Baptist revival, his newfound Christianity soon begins to chafe and bind, and so he begins a search for a more satisfying spirituality. Fortunately, as David would see it, his friend Fred, a lapsed Episcopal priest (the plot thickens!), sends him a book along with an encouraging note: "This is you. Read it slowly."

The book, as it turns out, is a copy of Pagels's *The Gnostic Gospels*. David opens the book and is immediately moved: "The fact that I was in tears by the time I finished the book's short introduction was the rawest reminder possible of my own fragility." David reads Jesus' statement, quoted by Pagels from one of the gnostic Gospels, "If you bring forth what is within you, what is within you will save you," and he is uplifted. "I thought I would levitate," he exclaims, "with this quote that early Christian leaders had decided to leave out of the Gospels from the discarded Gospel of Philip." But it is when David runs across the above-quoted teaching of Monoimus about finding God in yourself that his quest for true spirituality fizzes over:

> I paced the room like a forlorn geek in my underpants with sleet beating against the window. This was a form of Christianity where the church was not allowed to become a remote and dictatorial parent. My spine was still curved into a question mark but there was

the suggestion that remedies were close at hand rather than a matter of galactic communication.[40]

Aside from the seemingly painful condition of having one's spine
"curved into a question mark," David Burkett seems to be the whole
nine yards in terms of the new gnosticism. The church, as he has discovered, is a "remote and dictatorial parent" hiding the wonderful
secret words of Jesus in the *Gospel of Philip* under a rock so that true
seekers, like David, will be forced to drink from the official ecclesiastical spigot instead of being refreshed by the inner springs of spiritual
wisdom. The gnostic good news is that God is not "out there" sending
messages across the galaxy, but "close at hand," real close at hand, like
inside him, the divine flame burning in his soul. By the end of the
novel, Burkett has dubbed Pagels "Saint Pagels, my patron saint who
had reinvigorated the Christ who had died in my heart because He had
been encrusted to the point of suffocation with heinous doctrine."[41]

**4. An emphasis on present spiritual reality rather than eschatological
hope, on the God of timeless truth rather than the God who will
bring history to consummation.** For the ancient gnostics, the emphasis on the spiritual fullness of the present, on the "already," was so
strong that some commentators assumed that they lacked any future
eschatology and had no sense at all of the "not yet." A careful reading
of the Nag Hammadi texts, however, yields a more complex picture.[42]
Even so, the gnostic impulse operates essentially in the present tense. It
has an "instant eschatology," that is, the fullness of God is available to
the enlightened one now. The gnostic impulse grows suspicious of
eschatological talk about God's future victory, viewing this basically as
"pie in the sky" wishful thinking. In fact, a key difference between those
who are enlightened (those who have gnosis) and those who are not is
that the nonenlightened ignorantly look for hope in the future, rather
than in the present. The gnostic *Gospel of Thomas* expresses this anti-
eschatological view in a conversation between Jesus and his disciples:
"His disciples said to him, 'When will the rest for the dead take place,
and when will the new world come?' He said to them, 'What you are
looking forward to has come, *but you don't know it.*'"[43]

Taken separately, each of these four themes could be seen as simply an
alternative emphasis within traditional Christianity, a hue within the traditional Christian rainbow. For example, some Christians emphasize

more the external social world, but other Christians place the accent on the inner life. What makes this gnosticism, and not merely a lovely example of Christian pluralism, is the cumulative effect. Taken singly, none of these themes is particularly troublesome. Taken together, however, they shift the narrative grammar of the gospel, to borrow a helpful phrase from Cyril O'Regan. When combined into a coherent pattern, these four themes simply tell a different story than the gospel story. Given the cultural realities of our time, this story of a highly spiritualized faith that one acquires through knowledge and that puts one in direct and unmediated communion with God is quite appealing to many intelligent people. No one needs to be blamed or excommunicated for embracing it; no heresy trials need to be planned, but the gnostic impulse is a spectrum shift away from the gospel, and it should be addressed by Christian preachers.

In a time of biblical "illiteracy" and theological amnesia, many preachers are aware that they are preaching to congregations who do not remember the content of the Bible (if they ever knew it in the first place) and are not familiar with even the basic theological claims of the gospel. It would be a mistake, though, to imagine that we are preaching to blank tablets on which the gospel can be freshly inscribed. The culture has been scribbling on those tablets a religion of individual spiritual quest, and those who bring the gnostic impulse with them to church are less like catechumens needing to be taught and more like interfaith partners inviting dialogue between Christianity and another religion, a dialogue that often is already going on for them internally.

The phenomenon of gnostics in the pews of the church connects us strongly to the experience of the early church. For the most part, the first Christian gnostics were not schismatics; they were firmly inside the Christian community and not outside. They were not anti-Christians; they were Christians who saw things very, very differently. When the early church fathers took on the gnostics, they were not doing battle with a warring sect; they were wresting with brothers and sisters in the faith. "The typical gnostic," writes Phillip J. Lee, "was a member, often a pillar, of the local and recognized Christian Church."[44] Paul undoubtedly has some of them in mind when he says to the Corinthians, "If I have prophetic powers, and understand all mysteries and all knowledge (*gnōsis*) . . . but do not have love, I am nothing" (1 Cor. 13:2). Historian Arthur Darby Nock, in a classic essay on Christian gnosticism, noting that some of Paul's converts succumbed to the allure of gnosticism, added, "The plain truth is that you could not have found anyone in Corinth to direct you to a Gnostic church: the overwhelming probability

is that there was no such thing."[45] Gnostics weren't down the street lob-
bing grenades at the Christian church; they were at the Lord's Table
doing what all other Christians were doing: trying to figure out what this
all means.

In order to think more clearly and more closely about the gnostic
impulse, why it is appealing, what bright Christians find attractive about
it, what is at stake in it, and, ultimately, how to engage it in meaningful
dialogue, I want to explore in some detail the work of a theologian who
has been very influential among the new gnostics in the church, Marcus
J. Borg. I turn to this task in the next chapter.

4

Meeting Marcus Borg Again for the First Time

Faith seeking understanding . . .

—Anselm, *Proslogion*

The old morality was fond of the slogan 'faith seeking understanding';
the new morality believes that every yes and no must be a matter of
conscience.

—Van Harvey, *The Historian and the Believer*[1]

We cannot easily give our heart to something that our mind rejects.

—Marcus Borg, *The Heart of Christianity*[2]

Jewish theologian and philosopher Martin Buber once said that the true
enemy of faith is not *atheism*—the claim that there is no God—but
gnosticism—the claim that God can be intimately known.[3] If that is true,
American popular Christianity is constantly flirting, if not sleeping,
with the enemy. From the "come to Jesus" evangelistic rallies of Billy
Sunday and Billy Graham, to the overconfidence of fundamentalism to
know the truth, to the Christian self-help section of Barnes and Noble,
to the casual and chatty "chino and cappuccino" contemporary worship
services held in some churches, to the yearning to be deeply spiritual but
not religious, to the blandly reassuring "God loves you, God believes in
you" sermons that prevail in many pulpits, a too-immanent notion of
God underlies much of American Christianity. God is not seen as the
mysterium tremendum, an awesome and holy presence approached in
humility with eyes shielded and shoes off; God is viewed as the loqua-
cious next-door neighbor, always in a rocker on the porch, always near,
always accessible, always wanting to talk, and always eager to be *known*.

For all the quirky eccentricities of Harold Bloom's *The American
Religion,* he is on the right track to spot in much of mainstream American piety a religion that is "closer to ancient Gnostics than to early
Christians."[4] America, says Bloom, "is a religiously mad culture, furiously searching for the spirit,"[5] and whenever Americans get around to
homemade religious movements (e.g., the Mormons, Southern Baptists, and Pentecostals), they tend to celebrate the fact that "[t]he soul

stands apart, and something deeper than the soul, the Real Me or self or spark, thus is made free to be utterly alone with a God who is quite separate and solitary, that is a free God or God of freedom."[6]

Perhaps North American Christians are especially vulnerable to the gnostic siren song because, when it comes to figuring out whether faith should be focused *out there* on what God is doing in the world or *in here* on what God is doing in our hearts, we American Christians, of almost every theological stripe, tend to put our dime down on "in here," valuing above all—and there are liberal and conservative versions of this—a "personal relationship with Jesus." The old American revival hymn wonders about Jesus, "You ask me how I know He lives?" The hymn's answer breathes the claustrophobic air of American piety, "He lives within my heart."[7] A small space indeed for the Lord of all time and space. With our democratic and individualistic impulses, our entrepreneurial instincts, our revivalist past, and our current psychotherapeutic preoccupations, it is small wonder that the more inward, the more "sincere" Christian faith is deemed to be, the more we tend to prize it. Jeremy Lott spotted the gnostic streak that runs through American religion:

> The essence of the American Religion is "experiential." Few concessions are made to ancient ecclesial authority or tradition, and then only grudgingly. Such structures, in the minds of American believers, can only serve as impediments to the real point of religious experience, to wit, "being alone with God or with Jesus." . . . Moreover, this Jesus is different from the historical Jesus or the Christ of the Creeds. Rather, American Religionists yearn for that gnostic spark—that part of their soul that is older than creation itself—to be utterly alone with and to know a less challenging figure than the Jesus of the Gospel: "the American God or the American Christ."[8]

The New Testament is mindful of the inward power of the faith, but the gospel always makes it clear that the impact of the faith *in here,* in our hearts, is because of what God did *out there,* in God's mighty and redemptive acts. The writer of Ephesians, for example, stands in open-mouthed astonishment at what God has done *out there*: knocked down the seemingly permanent wall dividing Jew from Gentile, bringing Gentiles, who were once far away, near to God's promises, creating in the very self of God "one new humanity in place of the two, thus making peace" (Eph. 2:15b). Does this dramatic external event have an inward effect on believers? Yes, of course, but one that has some *size*:

I pray that you may have the power to comprehend, with all the saints, what is the breadth and length and height and depth, and to know the love of Christ that surpasses knowledge [that is, goes beyond gnosis], so that you may be filled with all the fullness of God. Now to him who by the power at work within us is able to accomplish abundantly far more than all we can ask or imagine, to him be glory in the church and in Christ Jesus to all generations, forever and ever. Amen. (Eph. 3:18–21)

The neo-gnostic impulse in contemporary Christianity that we described in the last chapter, while in most instances not qualifying as an "enemy of the faith" in Buber's sense, is still a basic rewriting of the Christian faith, a turning away from the God who is Other, the God of the scriptures, in favor of a highly spiritualized and always available God who is as close as our inward being, a God primarily conceived as a personal source of power and light within.

How does the God of mighty acts of salvation, narrated in scripture and sung in creed, become the downsized God of personal inspiration and inner illumination? How does the God of the Apostles' Creed, who created the heavens and the earth and raised Jesus from the dead, and whose Spirit calls the church into being and forges the communion of the saints, get replaced by the New Agey deity of the bland and narcissistic credo of John Shelby Spong?

> And
>   when you are accepted, accept yourself;
> when you are forgiven, forgive yourself;
> when you are loved, love yourself.
>   Grasp that Christpower
>   and dare to be
>   yourself![9]

The gnostic impulse does not spring up without cause, of course. But why now? Why do Spong, Borg, Pagels, and the other authors who succor the gnostic impulse have the ear of many in this generation of Christians, when a few decades ago their thought would have had little traction? Cyril O'Regan, in his book *Gnostic Return in Modernity*, is helpful; he points out that certain "ideological conditions" prevail whenever there is a revival of Christian gnostic thought.[10] The following list of these conditions is inspired by O'Regan, but I have modified his language in several ways and applied his categories to the contemporary

American religious scene (which he does not do).[11] This list, I believe, describes the weather pattern of our current cultural and ecclesial moment, a climate in which the gnostic impulse forms:

1. *Christian tradition is viewed as basically untrustworthy.* The sense prevails among many thoughtful Christians that the traditional ways of understanding the Christian faith are not only moribund but also deeply mistaken about how they describe God, redemption, and human life.

2. *Traditional Christianity is seen as especially failing the theodicy test.* Of all the grievances with traditional Christianity, one of the deepest dissatisfactions concerns how traditional Christianity fails to produce satisfactory responses to the problem of evil and the existence of innocent suffering.

3. *Christian eschatology has become implausible.* Traditional ways of talking about eschatology, the theology of hope and the "end things," have strained plausibility to the point of collapse. Many American Christians find literalistic descriptions of "heaven," life after death, and the second coming of Christ unbelievable, even vulgar, but do not have a working replacement eschatological vocabulary. Gnosticism, with its emphasis on timeless spirituality and its retreat from history, grows in the ruins of failed eschatologies.

4. *The core of the Christian faith is nevertheless worth saving.* Despite the fact that traditional Christianity is seen as mistaken and the scripture, conventionally interpreted, as damaging, there is still a refusal to give up on Christianity and the Bible. Instead, there is a mandate to revise Christianity and to change interpretive approaches to the Bible.

5. *Christianity is viewed as needing top-down revision, not small corrections.* Christianity needs to be revised not here and there, but wholly and completely. A new narrative of Christianity is proposed, one that contains all of the former elements but changes the traditional meanings of those elements.

6. *There is a hunger for a more "spiritual" interpretation of the scripture.* Doing this work of revision is seen to require fundamentally and dramatically changed patterns of biblical interpretation. Specifically, the Bible gets "saved" by shifting from literal readings to spiritual or metaphorical interpretations and by shifting from communal to more personal contexts of reading. The result is a new "master narrative" of scripture, in effect a "Bible behind

the Bible" that begins to take the place and status of the scripture itself.

7. *There is the conviction that profound differences exist between ordinary church people and those who deeply understand the spiritual truth of Christianity.* Despite a very high view of humanity in general and strong affirmations of the relationship between all human beings and God, there is still the notion that some people are spiritually elite, closer to the truth and to God by virtue of what they know. As regards the religious life, the Orwellian law holds: Everyone is equal, but some are more equal than others.

It is not much of a stretch to see in these seven conditions the essential characteristics of the "nasty suspicion" described in the last chapter—traditional ways of understanding the Christian faith are deeply mistaken and the language of the church has become obscurantist or even deceptive—and also an outline of a response to it: a from-the-ground-up revision of the Christian faith. When these seven meteorological conditions prevail in the church and in the culture in which it lives, a number of reactions could set in, but one likely weather forecast is for an increased chance of disillusionment on the part of intellectually keen Christians, followed by gnostic thunderstorms.

MARCUS BORG . . . AGAIN FOR THE FIRST TIME

But do these seven "weather conditions" actually show up in the writings of Spong, Borg, Pagels, Armstong, and the other authors who have had such an impact on the new spiritual quest in American Christianity? I believe they do, to different degrees, of course, and at different levels of scholarly analysis. In order to test that hunch and to point out graphic illustrations of the challenge of the gnostic impulse, I want to focus in this chapter on the work of one of these scholars: Marcus J. Borg, the popular author, lecturer, biblical scholar, and teacher, currently the Hundere Distinguished Professor of Religion and Culture at Oregon State University. I will refer occasionally to some of the other authors for emphasis or clarity, but I want to put the microscope on Borg's thought.

I choose to emphasize Borg's work for several reasons. First, the case can be made that, for church people, he has been the strongest and the most influential of these writers. He has lectured widely, not only on academic campuses but also in many congregations. His books are read and discussed in countless church settings, and he is quite effective in his goal of communicating a new way of seeing the Christian faith "to those for whom an earlier understanding makes little or no sense."[12] Many reflective Christians are persuaded that traditional ways of talking about the Christian faith have become intellectually untenable and that, for thinking people of faith, Borg is shining a light on the path that is both thoughtful and Christian. I have personally met a number of engaged and active Christians who say that the primary reason they have remained in the church is because of reading or hearing Marcus Borg.

Second, Borg has had a powerful impact on pastors and preachers. He shares much in common with those of us who are called to help articulate and build up the faith in a challenging culture. Borg is himself a committed Christian, one who has made his way over the years from a time of spiritual and intellectual exile back into the church. He has a passion to help Christians who are walking the same path that he has traveled, who feel alienated from their own religious tradition, who want a deeper faith. He understands the church and the ministry, and he grasps the struggles of both. The basic contours of Borg's personal story—moving from an evangelical and pious upbringing through an exile period of doubt and skepticism in adolescence to a new understanding of the faith as a young adult—could be told, with different details, by many, if not most, mainline clergy of Borg's generation.

Third, I am personally engaged and challenged by his books. He writes skillfully and compellingly. He speaks my language, inhabits the institutions I value, and brings sharp scholarly tools and apt categories to his work. He and I are products of a similar theological education; we have both "bit the apple" of historical criticism and know that we cannot return to a naive, precritical time before Christianity became historically conscious. We both share the goal of helping the church find the right language to express its faith and helping Christians live their faith with honesty and generosity in the contemporary world. I choose to look at Marcus Borg, not because he is so far away, but because he seems so very close.

Most of all, though, I want to examine Borg's thought because he presents one of the sharpest snapshots of what I have called the contemporary gnostic impulse in the church. I do not for a moment begrudge Borg the religious journey he has taken or the place at which he has arrived in his own understanding of Christianity, but, with all due respect, I do think that his personal faith manifesto, recorded across several of his popular books, is not a fully adequate map for other Christians who seek an authentic faith today or for the larger church. Many readers will recognize the title of this chapter as a play on the title of Borg's perhaps best-known work, *Meeting Jesus Again for the First Time.*[13] In this book, Borg wants to describe an ancient reality, the historical Jesus, to his readers in such a fresh and honest way that it will seem to them to be a new encounter. Just so, I think in Borg's writing we can perceive the return of something else quite ancient: not Jesus, but gnosticism—but this time wearing a new and attractive face. In Borg, we are meeting the gnostic impulse again for the first time.

This last claim discloses my main reason for choosing Borg's work for analysis. I am not so much interested in Borg per se but in the contemporary gnostics who are, I believe, out there in the pews of many congregations. If we can understand Borg, the way he thinks and why his approach to the Christian faith is so compelling to many people, then we can better understand the hungers, questions, and yearnings of these bright and motivated Christians who have the nasty suspicion that the church has not been telling them the whole truth and that the gospel we have been preaching is shallow and unsatisfying.

As a first step, let us review Borg's agenda in light of the seven conditions, stated above, for the return of the gnostic impulse. To begin, nothing could be clearer than the fact that Borg is convinced that traditional forms of Christianity are moribund and mistaken (condition #1). He is persuaded that Christianity has been dominated by an outmoded "earlier paradigm"—one that features literal modes of biblical interpretation, an emphasis on "believing now" as a means to achieve "salvation later," and a conviction that Christianity is the only true religion—but that this paradigm "no longer works" for many people.[14] Even so, Borg refuses to give up on the Bible or the Christian faith (condition #4). The Bible must be freed from literalistic modes of interpretation in favor of taking the Bible "metaphorically" and "sacramentally" (i.e., spiritually).[15]

Borg's biblical scholarship, particularly his Jesus research, produces not merely, as he would see it, better understandings of scripture, but also revised understandings of scripture that begin to float free from the originating biblical texts and take on a scripture-like status themselves (condition #6). Borg seeks "to go beneath the surface level of the gospels in order to discern the historical Jesus,"[16] a figure he calls "the pre-Easter Jesus." This Jesus, whom Borg has reconstructed through historical research, is, Borg says, "a remarkable and compelling figure, and our glimpses of him can provide content for what it means to take him seri-ously."[17] Despite his insistence that "both the historical Jesus and the canonical gospels matter to me as a Christian,"[18] it is clear that the pre-Easter, noncanonical Jesus holds the trump cards, and Borg's recon-struction of the hypothetical "pre-Easter Jesus" has a quasi-scriptural status and authority above the canonical Jesus. For example, Borg is con-vinced that the pre-Easter Jesus was not concerned about people "believ-ing in him," while the canonical Jesus, especially in the Gospel of John, is very much absorbed with the question of belief.[19] Borg opts clearly for the pre-Easter version. In short, the reconstructed "Bible behind the Bible" replaces and takes on the status of scripture.

Borg has a special concern to mute the New Testament language of eschatology (condition #3). The Gospels portray Jesus as an eschato-logical prophet, but not Borg's reconstruction. The pre-Easter Jesus was "noneschatological,"[20] he insists, which in Borg's view is a good thing, since popular Christianity's emphasis on God's future, heaven, and the afterlife constitute for Borg one "of Christianity's ten worst contribu-tions to religion."[21] Jesus, Borg says, "seems to have believed in an after-life, but he doesn't talk about it very much."[22] What James D. G. Dunn has said about the quest for the historical Jesus generally, applies also to Borg: "Characteristic of the quest is that it has been searching for a his-torical Jesus not simply behind but different from the Christ of faith, and different not simply from the Christ of faith but from the Jesus of the Gospels."[23]

Given the revolution of thought brought about by historical-critical approaches to scripture and early Christian history, Borg is convinced that there is no going back to a more innocent time when we simply took the Bible and the church fathers at their word. Christianity cannot be made plausible by piecemeal revisions. Borg points toward a com-pletely new way to envision Christianity, a major paradigm shift that provides a new and comprehensive way of "seeing Christianity as a whole"[24] (condition #5). An especially vexing problem with the earlier paradigm of Christianity, in Borg's view, is that it has an incoherent response to one of the most urgent theological problems facing con-temporary Christians: the presence of irrational evil and innocent suf-fering[25] (condition #2).

As for spiritual elitism (condition #7), it is only fair to say that Borg would be shocked to think that his views promote elitism of any kind. However, he does present a stark contrast between the "earlier" and "emerging ways" of being Christian. On the one hand, he wants to be evenhanded and make room for both, affirming diversity and saying that if the earlier paradigm "works for you," then go with it.[26] On the other hand, his heart doesn't seem in it. The "earlier paradigm" is committed to biblical literalism, is negative about women's ordination, views homosexuality as a sin, clings to a "monarchical" image of God that tends to reinforce a legalistic "performance model" of the Christian life, and holds to understandings of Jesus that are historically incorrect.[27] If viewing the earth as flat works for you, Borg seems to say, go with it, but what thinking, well-read Christian would? If we compare Borg's way of describing "traditional Christianity" with Borg's way of describing "emerging Christianity"—and if these are our only two choices—then smart, savvy, ethical Christians have but one choice. Christians who are more in tune with reality, more "in the know," Borg suggests, will tend to view God through the prism of a Spirit model, which is rich and free of the pollution of the current "domination system." Orwell was right: all are equal, but some are more equal than others.

A THREE-HANDED GAME

So we have seen that Borg's deep disenchantment with "traditional Christianity" and his revisionist program fit, like a hand in a glove, the "ideological conditions" for the revival of the gnostic impulse. But disenchantment and revisionism alone do not a gnostic make. That Borg has a strong distaste for traditional forms of Christianity and wants to knock the barnacles off of them does not ipso facto turn him into a cheerleader for gnosticism. It may mean only that he is a liberal Christian, or it may mean even something as bland as that he is a Protestant. In order to see the tacit gnostic impulse at work in Borg's writing, we need to get deeper into the grain of his thought.

When we do, I think it gradually becomes clear that Borg's theological position has often been misread, by both his fans and his critics. Typically, the story of contemporary American Christianity, especially Protestantism, has been told as a chronic tug-of-war between two forces—orthodoxy, on the one hand, and liberalism, on the other—each side changing and maturing over time as a result of the struggle. As a popular theologian, Borg has usually been seen as a levelheaded and straight-shooting star player for the liberal team, or, as he sometimes prefers to describe it, for "progressive Christianity." Borg himself reinforces this impression by characteristically dividing tough, controversial issues into two clearly marked positions, roughly progressive versus orthodox. For example, he speaks of the "earlier Christian paradigm" (orthodox) versus "an emerging Christian paradigm" (progressive),[28] "a belief-centered way of being Christian" (orthodox) versus "a transformation-centered way of being Christian" (progressive),[29] and a "monarchical model of God" (orthodox) versus a "Spirit model of God" (progressive).[30] Having divided the world into two options, orthodox and progressive, Borg sometimes makes sympathetic and understanding comments about the orthodox position, but it is plain that his loyalties finally lie on the other side. In sum, Borg appears to both friend and foe to be a scholarly liberal fighting—gently and empathetically, but fighting nonetheless—against an encrusted orthodoxy.

But what if the basic contest is not between some static orthodoxy, on the one side, and some freewheeling liberalism, on the other, but is much more multifaceted, fluid, and dynamic? If for the sake of sorting out the issues we need to name sides, then I think O'Regan is correct to identify not two main combatants—orthodoxy versus liberalism—but three: orthodoxy versus liberalism versus gnosticism redux.[31] Orthodoxy is the bête noir for both liberals and gnostics, and because gnosticism and liberalism have a common enemy and score many of the same points, from a distance they can appear indistinguishable. But gnosticism is actually quite a different force and system of thought from liberalism. With three teams on the field, the lines of engagement are often confused, and there is a great deal of intermingling of players. Indeed, what is intriguing—and often confusing—about Borg is that, at any given moment, he can come off the bench for any of the three teams.

Borg, as we have said, is typically viewed as a historically savvy proponent of liberal Christianity, and there is much about him that does indeed fit this bill. As liberalism is wont to do, he is constantly on a mission to make Christianity intellectually respectable by bringing it into conversation with and correlation to (and some would charge, co-option by) contemporary science, history, and philosophy. Like most classical liberals, he trusts the results of the historical critical method as applied to the investigation of the Bible and other Christian sources. Also, Borg, like other liberals from the nineteenth century forward, is less interested in the Christ of church dogma and claims to be more attracted to the "Jesus of history"—his life, his ethical stands, and even his faith and personality.

Intriguingly, though, Borg also shows the markings of orthodoxy, even though he would probably be quite surprised to hear himself described as an advocate for "the earlier paradigm." After all, it has been many years since he left behind the conservative Scandinavian Lutheran church of his youth, where he was given the old tapes that "Jesus was the divinely begotten Son of God who died for the sins of the world and whose message was about himself and his saving purpose and the importance of believing in him."[32] But has Borg really left this behind? It is striking how much of his writing is placed over against and defined by the religion of his childhood, which means, of course, that orthodox piety continues to draw the lines on the playing field and set the terms of the debate. Borg may chafe at ideas like the divinity of Jesus, the doctrine of sin, and the necessity of proper belief, but he cannot really spring free of them, and for all his talk of an "emerging paradigm," these older themes remain as the master categories that must be addressed and that consequently shape his work. Also, the old personal piety is not quite dead in Borg. Borg, the methodical Jesus historian, still has the capacity to throw over all objectivity in favor of falling in love with a romantic portrait of Jesus.

But even though Borg has some lingering hints of orthodoxy and some strong tendencies toward characteristic liberalism, when the dust clears and the game is done, I see Borg essentially as wearing the colors of the gnostic team, a case I will make in more detail below. A generous reading of Borg would see that much of his power and appeal comes from the fact that he pulls together and even synthesizes these disparate strands in contemporary Christianity: the piety of orthodoxy, the honest intellectual inquiry of liberalism, and the spirituality of gnosticism. A less sympathetic take would say that Borg's theology has a certain homeless quality as he wanders from position to position. Perhaps it goes with the territory of being an academic who writes for the popular religious public, but he seems at times unsure of his constituency, unclear about the contours of his own thought, desirous of boldly slaying the dragon of traditional Christianity but still being welcomed at the church picnic. Borg seems to want to come across as the clear-eyed and rational historian who can, with one deft slice of the scalpel and without hesitation or regret, cut away churchly accretions to the historical Jesus, but also as one who is in this business because he loves Jesus passionately and has had nonrational experiences of nature mysticism.

Seeming contradictions abound in Borg, often making it difficult to assess the patterns of his thought. For example, in one book Borg says, as we noted earlier, that he thinks that popular Christianity's emphasis on the afterlife was a terrible idea,[33] but later in the same book he spends several compelling pages wondering whether we'll know our loved ones in the afterlife and whether the afterlife might involve reincarnation and/or purgatory.[34] Borg warns us that the Gospels "are not divine products inspired directly by God whose contents therefore are to be believed,"[35] but he also assures us that, "The Bible is for us as Christians our sacred scripture, our sacred story."[36] He expresses his distaste for eschatological thinking as a corruption of the biblical emphasis on salvation in *this* world,[37] and then later cites scripture as evidence of Christianity's hope for the future redemption of the whole of creation,[38] only to pull back again ever so slightly from the whole idea of a future consummation.[39] It is difficult with precision to know how Borg organizes his thought, what counts as primary and what is secondary and derived from first-order claims. We think we have it when Borg argues that the historical Jesus, who stands behind the biblical text, is central to Christianity. All right, then, if the historical Jesus is central, then everything else radiates out from that phenomenon. But, no, Borg also maintains at various times that the Bible is "central," God is "central," the kingdom of God is "central," the transformation of self and world is "central," faith is "central," seeing life as a whole is "central," open hearts and spiritually "thin places" are "central," and life in the Spirit is "central." Central is a crowded place in Borg's theology.

But even though there is some marshy ground in Borg's overall scheme and one can find confusing places and spots where he seems to contradict himself, the basic contours of his thought are clear enough. Let's get out the tweezers, then, and see if we can identify the strands in Borg's approach that connect him to the gnostic impulse.

MEETING THE GNOSTIC JESUS AGAIN
FOR THE FIRST TIME

In the last chapter, we named four main themes of the gnostic impulse. Let us view Borg's thought through the prism of these themes.

1. Humanity is "saved" by gnosis. In classical gnosticism, as Birger Pearson says, "saving gnosis comes by revelation from a transcendent realm, mediated by a revealer who has come from that realm in order to awaken people to a knowledge of God and a knowledge of the true nature of the human self."[40] Perhaps few contemporary Christians would recognize themselves in that statement, but many Christian today fully subscribe to the underlying idea that what makes people whole is not repentance and forgiveness but acquiring a certain kind of spiritual knowledge, learning the truth about God and about their authentic selves. This is the gnostic conviction that *humanity is saved by gnosis,* or as Spong expresses it, "We are not fallen sinners who need to be rescued; we are incomplete creatures who need to be empowered to step into the new possibilities of an expanding life."[41]

A quick sampling of church Web sites under the "what we believe" or "mission statement" sections discloses an abundance of saved-by-knowledge language. "Love is the doctrine of this church; the quest of truth its sacrament," reads one such statement, which goes on to describe the congregation's spiritual goal in language that could be lifted from a gnostic tract: "to seek knowledge in freedom, to serve humanity in fellowship, to the end that all souls shall grow into harmony with the divine." Another church asserts "that each of us has a right and responsibility to support one another as we search for the divine by living, learning, and growing," while yet another affirms that the church believes "that God is most clearly known where diverse people seek new insights, question hurtful assumptions, employ a multiplicity of images for the Divine, and create a warm, welcoming community in the name of Jesus Christ."

All of these statements need to be taken, of course, with a grain of salt. They are, after all, merely homespun theological concoctions, probably hammered out by beleaguered committees in between approving budgets and deciding whether to fire yet another youth minister. What is interesting about them, though, is the commonplace but seemingly unquestioned notion that the best way to describe Christianity is as a way to get *knowledge,* a religious achievement that we accomplish on our own steam, mainly learning wise things about God that will make us better, more spiritual people.

Christians historically have claimed that the essential human problem is not lack of knowledge but a lack of will. It is not that we have momentarily misplaced the map of life and need to stop in at a spiritual convenience store for directions, but that we, as the classic prayer puts it, have "erred and strayed from your ways like lost sheep, and we have followed too much the devices and desires of our own hearts." The human problem is twofold: we don't know the way to full human life, but even if someone told us the way, we have a deep proclivity not to follow it. So we need not only knowledge, but also repentance and redemption. Thus Christians have said that the gospel is not primarily

about our quest for God, but God's quest for us. God's rescue of alienated and broken humanity. As the Nicene Creed states: "For us and for
our salvation he came down from heaven; by the power of the Holy
Spirit he became incarnate from the Virgin Mary, and was made man."

But it is these very ideas—humanity as sinful, Jesus as the incarnate
savior—that many thoughtful Christians find implausible, and in these
typical congregational mission statements there is a completely different
worldview. The basic human dilemma, they seem to say, is not that we
are in trouble and need to be rescued, not that we are sinners who cannot muscle our own way to wholeness because we are captive to powers
that overwhelm us, not that we are "prone to wander, Lord, I feel it,
prone to leave the God I love," but that we are good, well-intentioned
people who yearn with all our hearts to be one with God and lack only
the proper illumination to get there. We need a spiritual education, the
knowledge and guidance of holy truth, to make our way toward union
with the divine. We don't need to repent; we need to go to spiritual
school. As Philip Lee points out, the gnostic impulse replaces *mea culpa*
("I have sinned") with *mea ignorantia* ("I didn't know").[42] (My favorite
of the church Web sites I discovered had a button on the home page
labeled "What We Believe." When I clicked on it, it took me to a page
that said, "Under construction. Come back later.")

What Borg says about all this, about the human condition and
divine salvation, cannot be neatly arranged into a systematic statement.
In the main, though, his thoughts about these matters seem to spring
from a dramatic discovery he made in a seminary New Testament
course. "There I learned that the image of Jesus from my childhood—
the popular image of Jesus as the divine savior who knew himself to be
the Son of God and who offered up his life for the sins of the world—
was not historically true."[43] Just as an aside, as important as this insight
is to Borg, it is not readily apparent what this statement might mean.
What does it mean that this childhood image of Jesus is *not historically
true*? If Borg had said, "I no longer believe in the Jesus of my childhood,
the Jesus who was a divine savior who knew thus and so about himself
and did such and such," that would be one thing, but Borg doesn't
present this as a confessional statement, but as historical fact. Borg
seems to be saying that he discovered in seminary the mind-boggling
truth that historians are absolutely certain that Jesus—the actual Jesus
who walked around Palestine, as opposed to the storied and theologically interpreted Jesus of the New Testament—did not think of himself
as the Son of God and did not construe the meaning of his life as an

offering for the world's sins, and so we need to figure out a new and better way to understand Jesus and what he was about.

Now this may be so; the possibility can be entertained that Jesus may, as a matter of fact, have never thought of himself as anything close to a Son of God or as a savior, and any Christian who wants to base faith on these ideas is off on a snipe hunt. But in order to claim that we know this as historical "fact," a historian would have to have access to the interior thoughts and consciousness of the man Jesus (which, of course, no historian has), or would have to demonstrate that the whole "Son of God and savior" business could not possibly have been in Jesus' repertoire because it postdates him (which it doesn't), or would have to find documentary evidence from Jesus' own pen stating something like, "Despite what my followers think and say, I do not imagine myself to be the Son of God or anybody's savior" (which, as far as we know, doesn't exist).

The point is that Borg seems to misunderstand, or at least misstate, what he learned in that New Testament course. A historian, strictly as a historian, has no way at this distance to make such a claim about Jesus' self-consciousness or vocational self-understanding. What Borg is really saying, I think (and this helps us understand the gnostics in the pews today) is that, in the light of a certain kind of biblical scholarship, he *no longer finds it persuasive or plausible* to imagine that the actual, historical Jesus was much like the picture of Jesus Borg was taught as a child, namely the Jesus who was the self-conscious Son of God who understood himself to be dying for the sins of the world.

Lurking in the background of all this for Borg (and this also tunes us in to the gnostics in congregations) are the powerful and negative religious memories and understandings of his childhood, where "sin" was doing bad things that made God really angry and made one feel guilty, and where Jesus was something like God disguised in a human body and a bathrobe who could, if he wished, have said things like, "I am very God of very God, the Pantocrator, and, if you'll step aside, I am on my way to Jerusalem to be tried by Pontius Pilate and to die on a cross for the redemption of your miserable sins." Never mind that this comes nowhere near what "traditional Christianity" has confessed. If this is the way the gospel was taught in that Dakota Lutheran church in the 1940s, no wonder Borg flees the sanctuary, screaming that this cannot possibly be true, and grabs onto the skirts of "history" for protection.

The main issue for us here, however, is not what portion of his childhood faith Borg has cast aside as "not historically true," but instead what he has put in its place. He sings a tune hummed by many others

in the church today when he says that what the church taught him as a
child cannot be true and that we need some new, more truthful vision of
Jesus. As a Jesus historian, Borg has joined with others in the "recon-
struction" of a historical Jesus who has, to them, more credibility than
the Jesus of Borg's youth. We shall have more to say about this later, but
at this point it is important to see that the Jesus who manages to squeeze
through the mesh of Borg's historical filters is not the doctrinally
enhanced "messiah" or "savior" but a much more approachable, down-
to-earth "sage." "Jesus was a teacher of wisdom," Borg says, adding,
"This is the strongest consensus among today's Jesus scholars."

As a sage, Jesus' primary role was naturally to teach gnosis, wisdom,
"a transformation of perception . . . [that] flowed out of his own spiritual experience."[44] The purpose of this teaching, Borg says, was to help
people move from "secondhand religion," which for us is "thinking that
the Christian life is about believing what the Bible says or what the doctrines of the church say," to "firsthand religion," namely, a direct relationship to "the reality that we call God."[45]

2. A focus on the spiritual inner self, the "divine spark" within. The
reason why we can aspire to a direct relationship to God, unmediated
by church, doctrine, or other structure, is that, to pick up the themes of
the gnostic impulse again, when we focus on the spiritual inner self we
get in touch with our origins in God, the "divine spark" within. Borg
tells the oft-repeated story of the parents of a three-year-old girl who
overhear her saying to her newborn brother in the crib, "Tell me about
God—I've almost forgotten."[46] This story, Borg says, "is both haunting
and evocative," because it conveys the truth that "we come from God"
but that in the process of growing up we lose our innocence and forget
"the one from whom we came and in whom we live. The birth and
intensification of self-consciousness, self-awareness, involves a separa-
tion from God."[47]

This is Borg's updated version of the traditional doctrine of "the
fall." In the classical description of the fall, involving the Genesis story
of the disobedience of Adam and Eve, humanity commits an act of
defiance. Here, though, the fall is a loss of gnosis; it is a fall that takes
place entirely within our minds, inside our consciousness. We used to
remember Eden, we used to be at one with God, but growing up caused
us to forget all this, and as a consequence we are separated from God.
Thus, Borg says, we need to be "born again," which is "the way to
recover our true self, the path to beginning to live our lives from the

inside out rather than the outside in."[48] How does this happen? Through the midwifery of spirituality, which Borg defines as "*becoming conscious of and intentional about a deepening relationship with God.*"[49]

Born again by becoming conscious and intentional about a deepening relationship with God? The main action of redemption takes place, then, on a very small stage: the spiritual inner self. Salvation becomes a return to the divine from which we came, the placing again of the burning coal of our spirit into the originating fire of God.

3. An antipathy toward incarnation and embodiment. The early Christian gnostics were not only convinced that gnosis, wisdom, leads to redemption; they had also drunk deeply from the well of Neoplatonism and viewed the creation, the material world, not as the work of the transcendent God of light, but rather as the work of an inferior deity. This was, for them, not merely playing around with divine myths, but was a result of their outrage over the suffering and evil they saw all around them. How could the true God have created something as corrupt as the material world? The answer? God didn't create this world at all; a lower deity is responsible.

This division between higher and lower gods was paralleled by a corresponding split in human beings. Human bodies and coarse emotions belong to "this world," to the lower material reality, but minds and spirits are part of the transcendent God, from which they came and to which they yearn to return.[50] Whenever the early Christian preachers began to speak about material reality, bodies, and flesh—about creation, incarnation, the resurrection of the body—the early gnostics recoiled.

While the vast majority of contemporary Christians would find meaningless the ancient gnostic talk of two gods, demiurges, and lesser deities, there is nevertheless embedded in the gnostic impulse a lingering bias against materiality, flesh, and embodiment. The true faith is spiritual, the true God is Spirit, the true gospel is unbounded and universal. Whenever anything with walls, structures, or flesh—such as a church building, an institution, a creed, a human body, other people—comes lumbering on the scene, the spiritual temperature drops precipitously. As the contemporary hymn says, with a whiff of gnosticism, "Not in the dark of buildings confining, not in some heaven, light-years away, but here in this place the new light is shining."[51] Or as Borg complains about secular culture, "Our culture's secular wisdom does not affirm the reality of the Spirit; the only reality about which it is certain is the visible world of our ordinary experience."[52]

But what about "the visible world of our ordinary experience"? Is it right to separate this from "the reality of the Spirit"? Christian theology is actually quite nuanced on this point, refusing finally to pit the world of the Spirit against the world of material reality. The New Testament writers were able to distinguish between viewing the world *kata sarka*, that is, "according to the flesh," and *en sarki*, that is, "in the flesh." To regard the world *kata sarka* is to see it only from a human, "fleshy" point of view, to reduce life to the merely material, only what we can touch and see. Paul says that humanity once even saw Christ *kata sarka* but that now, because of the new creation wrought in Christ, faith no longer sees anyone or anything *kata sarka* (2 Cor. 5:16–17). But this does not mean that Christians turn away from the material world into the world of pure Spirit. No, instead of seeing everything *kata sarka*, we now see the presence and activity of God *en sarki*, in the visible and material world of ordinary experience. The New Testament warns us not to be distracted by blather about spirituality, because not everything that claims to be "spiritual" is actually of the Spirit. Indeed, we are to "test the spirits to see whether they are of God," and, as strange as it may seem, one test of the spirits is to see how seriously they take the flesh: "[E]very spirit that confesses that Jesus Christ has come in the flesh [*en sarki*] is from God" (1 John 4:2).

This "in the flesh" claim in Christianity is quite important. Christianity is insistently incarnational—"the Word became *flesh* and lived among us" (John 1:14)—which is not just an ex post facto doctrinal encrustation imposed on Jesus the Spirit man, the wisdom teacher. It is in fact deep wisdom itself, namely, that counter to many religious visions ancient and contemporary, the spiritual life is not to be achieved by transcending this world and ascending into some ethereal immaterial realm of the spirit. To the contrary, this is the world that God has made, this is the creation God called "very good," and it is in this world that God has chosen to dwell. The spiritual life for a Christian is not a rising above place and circumstance. The irony of Christian spiritual life is that it is always and in every way material. It *is* hassling with these particular people who make up my actual life and being in these relationships and raising these children and picking up this plow and being a good steward of this money and that land and suffering through this loss and rejoicing over these mercies and trying to live in peace with those neighbors and dwelling in this community and dealing with that political tangle and confessing this creed and building up these institutions and seeking in the midst of all of this messiness to serve the Jesus Christ who did not come as an idea or as a principle or as a spiritual experience but in the middle of the very same material muck and mire and "in the flesh."

In the world of pop spirituality, we see a clear expression of the gnostic animus against embodiment and incarnation in the so-called "Conversations with God" held by Neale Donald Walsch, which he has turned into a number of best-selling books and videos. Walsch claims to have received, during a troubled time in his life, messages or "conversations" from a rather chatty God. Based on the content of these conversations, it would seem that "God," just like Walsch himself, has had it up to here with embodied, "organized religion." What a coincidence! Let's listen in:

Walsch: Do we need to return to religion? Is that the missing link?

God: Return to spirituality. Forget about religion . . .

Walsch: Why do You say, forget religion?

God: Because it is not good for you. Understand that in order for organized religion to succeed, it has to make people believe they *need* it. In order for people to put faith in something else, they must first lose faith in themselves. So the first task of organized religion is to make you lose faith in yourself. The second task is to make you see that *it* has the answers you do not. And the third and most important task is to make you accept its answers without question. If you question, you start to think! If you think, you start to go back to that Source Within. . . . I will have you be like me.

Walsch: But we can't be like You. That would be blasphemy.

God: Ah . . . blasphemy is that you have been taught such things by the church. I tell you this; you have been made in the image and likeness of me. It's the destiny you came to fulfill.[53]

Walsch is, of course, a poseur who has the chutzpah to place his own sloppy ravings about spirituality in the mouth of God, but he does come by his rant against organized religion honestly. His mother, a Wisconsin Roman Catholic, rarely went to church. When a youthful Walsch challenged her about this, she replied in good gnostic fashion, "I don't have to go to church. God comes to me."[54]

Borg does not stoop to the trivial level of Walsch. Interestingly, though, if Walsch plays off of a gnostic distaste for embodiment and "institutional religion," Borg does speak, albeit in a more sophisticated and scholarly way, to the same impulse. Borg would protest that, to the contrary, he advocates for participation in the real, embodied, institutional church and in its concrete practices, but a closer examination raises questions about this.

There are several places to catch glimpses of Borg's distrust of embodiment. The first is in his view of God. As is his customary method, Borg presents for his readers two starkly contrasting views of God: the old stuff, "supernatural theism," which imagines God as "*a personlike being,*" and Borg's revised stuff, "panentheism," which "imagines God as the *encompassing Spirit* in whom everything that is, is."[55] Borg opts, obviously, for the latter, which allows him further to define God, in a sort of soft Tillichian fashion, as "the most common name for 'what is,' for 'ultimate reality,' for 'the ground of being,' for 'Being itself,' for 'isness.'"[56]

Borg chooses panentheism for several reasons. First, he believes it overcomes supernatural theism's tendency to see God anthropomorphically, as a real existing Being out there beyond the world—in supernatural theism's more vulgar forms, a God with a mouth to speak, hands to intervene in human affairs, and gendered parts to insure the maleness of absolute authority. At this point we already become nervous, wondering just who Borg has in his sights here. Is there any thinking person over the age of five who actually conceives of God in the literalistic fashion of this supernatural theism? Is this the dragon of Borg's childhood piety now needing to be slain? Borg's supernatural theism seems more of a caricature, a label for a blend between childishness and deism. I am reminded of Terry Eagleton's response to Richard Dawkins's *The God Delusion:*

> [Dawkins] seems to imagine God, if not exactly with a white beard, then at least as some kind of chap, however supersized. He asks how this chap can speak to billions of people simultaneously, which is rather like wondering why, if Tony Blair is an octopus, he has only two arms. For Judeo-Christianity, God is not a person in the sense that Al Gore arguably is. Nor is he a principle, an entity, or 'existent': in one sense of that word it would be perfectly coherent for religious types to claim that God does not in fact exist. He is, rather, the condition of possibility of any entity whatsoever, including ourselves. He is the answer to why there is something rather than nothing. God and the universe do not add up to two, any more than my envy and my left foot constitute a pair of objects.[57]

The point is that even those thoughtful theologians who do not number themselves among the panentheists do not imagine God as some Being among beings, a God to whom one should pray, as the priest does in Monty Python's *The Meaning of Life,* "Oh Lord . . . Oooh you are so big . . . so absolutely huge . . . Gosh, we're all really impressed down here I can tell you."

Borg also imagines that panentheism gets rid of the idea of a God who intervenes. To Borg, adherents of supernatural theism believe God intervened in Jesus' birth, Jesus' miracles, Jesus' death, and Jesus' resurrection, and continues to intervene today. It seems to me that Borg confuses two distinct theological ideas here: *intervention*, which implies that God is completely outside of the world, in "heaven" perhaps, and reaches in from the outside to make changes in earthly history, and *divine action*, a belief that God is an agent acting in the world and that events cannot be fully described without reference to God's activity.

Human beings do not have many meaningful ways to describe divine action, and one of the best is to draw analogies to human action and agency. Thus the Bible uses language for divine action that sounds a lot like intervention—God hardened Pharaoh's heart, God spoke to Moses, God sent the angel Gabriel to Mary, and so on. But no thoughtful theologian from Paul forward has taken such statements at literal face value. Borg wants to get rid of naive ideas of divine intervention—and who doesn't?—but he actually manages to erase the concept of divine action in the process. For Borg, the claim that God never intervenes is virtually equivalent to the claim that God never acts (which creates much mischief for him, including an incoherent passage where he bends over backward to explain why he finds petitionary and intercessory prayer to be a meaningful practice, even though he disavows the only two reasons why this could be so, namely, either prayer somehow psychologically heals the heart of the one who prays or prayers are petitions addressed to a God who genuinely hears and responds[58]). Other panentheist theologians have creative and interesting ways of describing divine action, but the category is still very much present for them.[59]

Borg is also persuaded that a panentheistic image of God sidesteps the difficulties that traditional theism runs into with theodicy. "If God could have intervened to stop the Holocaust but chose not to," he asks, "what kind of sense does that make? . . . To suppose that God intervenes implies that God does so for some, but not for others."[60] One is tempted to make two impertinent responses here. One is to point out that outrage over suffering in creation is what caused the first Christian gnostics to attribute creation not to the "real" and spiritual God but to that infe-rior, materialistic God of the Old Testament, and here we go again. The second, and more churlish response to Borg's question is to say yes, the biblical story does indeed imply that God is free to act for some and not for others—just ask Cain, just ask the Egyptian charioteers, just ask Job—and who are we to puff out our moral chests and impose our little notions of fairness and democracy on God? But that's not the point.

Peevishness aside, though, the main point is that all forms of theol-ogy—theism, panentheism, liberation theology, what-have-you—have problems making sense out of innocent suffering on a grand scale. The only position that does not have a theodicy problem is atheism, and that just moves the issue over to the existential and philosophical regis-ters. One wonders finally if Borg's version of panentheism is really any better than the crudest theism on the suffering issue. Borg's God is "the encompassing Spirit in whom everything that is, is. The universe is not separate from God, but *in* God." Taking Borg at his word here, his eagerness to bring God and the universe into such intimate relationship has the unfortunate side effect, not of avoiding the theodicy problem, but of bringing the Holocaust, children dying of melanoma, HIV-AIDS, and the like right into the very life of God.

The upshot of Borg's view of God is that God is now so vague, so amorphous, as to lack all definition. The biblical God is a God who acts, who broods, who loves and rages with jealousy, who hears the cries of the oppressed with compassion, and who even on occasion repents. This is a God whose arc touches human life in tangible ways, who gets involved in the stuff of the world. A God who must be narrated to be known, who can be sung about and conversed with. A God who has a name and who walks in the garden in the cool of the day. Gnostics don't like this God. Too much embodiment, too much materiality. Better to be in relationship with the no-name God who is "isness."

We can also see Borg's aversion to embodiment in his understanding of history and culture. Although Borg is himself a New Testament his-torian, curiously history tends to function for him as a negative or dis-qualifying category. "[T]he longer I studied the Christian tradition," he writes, "the more transparent its human origins became. Religions in general (including Christianity), it seemed to me, were manifestly cul-tural products. I could see how their readily identifiable psychological and social functions served human needs and cultural ends. The notion that we made it all up was somewhat alarming, but also increasingly compelling."

This is a very interesting statement. All thoughtful students of religion know, of course, that religions have "human origins" and are "cultural products." Unless one imagines a God who drops the book of Leviticus out of the sky and bellows from heaven, "There's your religion. Now do it!" what else could religions be but cultural products woven from social and psychological strands? Borg, however, seems to assume here that wherever one finds human fingerprints on religion, it is a disqualifier because it flattens it out as *only* human. There is little acknowledgment of what classical Christianity has not only claimed but celebrated and trumpeted from the housetops, that God could be working out divine purposes precisely in and through the messiness of history and culture. No, if we catch actual people and their "human needs and cultural ends" involved, then we must have "made it all up."

Borg is more thoughtful theologically than to hold completely to this view of history and culture. The paragraph quoted above is Borg's description of a discovery he made in his younger days, and there are other places in his writing where he nuances this view. But the idea that historical realities and cultural forms are at best compromises and at worst corruptions haunts Borg's work. Take for example Borg's view of religious pluralism. He says that all religions are "institutions." They have "external forms," such as scriptures, rituals, practices, and organizational structures. Religions have "traditions," which are themselves types of institutions. "Religion," Borg says, "is 'organized religion.'"[61]

Sure, but what do we do with this insight that religion is inevitably institutionalized activity? On the one hand, Borg wants to recognize the external forms of religion as good and necessary. Spirituality needs religion as education needs schools. Religion is the means by which "spirituality gains traction,"[62] and we should respect the different external forms and rituals of other religions as "sacraments of the sacred."[63] On the other hand, Borg seems to think of religious traditions as accidental structures temporarily containing a purer, freer spiritual reality. Religions have external forms, he says, but there is an "internal core," which is "the heart of religion, . . . the experience of the sacred, 'the real,' 'the More.'" Religions are like cardboard boxes. They come in all shapes and sizes, but they all contain a similar internal core.[64]

At first glance, this seems like a wonderful way to express the nature of religious traditions. It knocks out fundamentalism with a single blow and makes interfaith dialogue a happy experience. We have differently shaped egg cartons, but essentially we're all holding the same spiritual eggs. Behind this easy ecumenism, though, is the gnostic impulse that bodies are but mere containers for the real stuff, namely, the spirit. The Christian doctrine of incarnation, however, challenges simplistic divisions between bodies and spirits. God is Spirit, but we have come to encounter and know this Spirit most fully in the flesh-and-blood Jesus of Nazareth. The painstaking development of creedal affirmations about the two natures of Christ may look to freethinking spiritual seekers as so much authoritarian bombast, but it actually reflects the church's passionate desire to keep people from driving off the mountain by thinking that spirituality can ever be spoken of apart from embodiment.

Whatever else one may say about baptism, the Lord's Supper, the scriptures, creeds, and practices of the Christian faith, they are not simply our particular culturally shaped external forms for carrying some universal sacred, gaseous, spiritual More. They are in their form and shape, in their embodiment, bound up inextricably with the holy reality to which they point. This is true of other religious traditions as well, which is part of what makes interfaith dialogue so difficult, complex, vexing, controversial, and ultimately promising and rewarding.

We can also see Borg's shyness about embodiment in his understanding of Jesus. Borg earned his spurs as a historian of Jesus, which at first glance would seem to suggest that he is very much into the embodied, actual, historical Jesus rather than the theology-encrusted, imagined, and abstracted Jesus he finds in the formaldehyde suspension of later church doctrine. But look more closely. Borg, a member of the Jesus Seminar, aims his methodology at separating the "pre-Easter Jesus," that is, the actual, historical Jesus, from the "post-Easter Jesus," the Jesus as interpreted and reinterpreted by the church. But there is a methodological problem right at the outset. Virtually 100 percent of the early written material we have about Jesus was composed by people of faith, that is, everything we know about Jesus was written by the post-Easter Christians. How can we separate out the pre-Easter stuff when the whole lot is post-Easter?

New Testament scholar Richard Hays tells about a message his lawyer brother left on his answering machine after the brother heard an interview on NPR with a member of the Jesus Seminar. Hays's brother, it seems, was astonished to learn that these scholars had published a new version of the Gospels purporting to show what Jesus *really* said. "How can they claim to know what Jesus really said or didn't say?" Hays's brother roared into the answering machine. "I have enough trouble proving in a court of law what somebody said six months ago! Should I take this book seriously?"[65]

The idea that we could, with a high degree of confidence, sift out the pre-Easter wheat from the post-Easter chaff is ambitious to the point of hubris. This is not to say that some good, but modest, guesswork cannot be done, and in fact biblical scholarship has been making these educated guesses about the historical Jesus for a couple of centuries now. The way it is done is to formulate some rules and guidelines and then to apply them systematically to the biblical material. For example, a biblical scholar might decide that whenever the Gospel writers report a statement in the mouth of Jesus that would have been awkward for the later church, it should be given a greater probability of authenticity, because it is unlikely that the later church would have made up embarrassing material. Fair enough, so long as we guard against the inherent danger of circular reasoning: deciding in advance that embarrassing Jesus statements are more likely to be authentic can result in the "discovery" of only what we decided to look for, a "historical" Jesus who says mainly embarrassing things.

The upshot of all this is an uncomfortable little secret of historical Jesus research. The Jesus historian bravely announces that he is going to find the "real" Jesus snuggled under all those post-Easter blankets, but the only way to go about this is to do some imagining in advance about what the "real" Jesus is like and then go looking for him. The Jesus that Borg finds has a curious trait: this Jesus, unlike the Judaism out of which he came and more like gnosticism, hasn't much interest in eschatology.

4. An emphasis on present spiritual reality rather than eschatological hope, on the God of timeless truth rather than the God who will bring history to consummation. Borg assumes in advance that the pre-Easter Jesus was nonmessianic (that is, he didn't think of himself as the Messiah or the Son of God) and noneschatological (which Borg takes to mean that Jesus did not think the end of the world was coming in his own generation).[66] And voilà! The pre-Easter Jesus that Borg finds is neither messianic nor eschatological.

This business of assuming something and then finding it is, of course, circular reasoning, and Borg knows of this circularity in historical Jesus research. He compares the historian to a detective who gathers and analyses the evidence on the way to making a hunch about the crime. "A detective's work," he admits, "thus involves a kind of circularity. So also does the work of a historian." The historian forms a hunch and then looks back at the evidence to see if it fits. The proof in the pudding, though, is "what the jury makes of the reconstruction, whether it strikes them as persuasive or not."[67]

It is precisely on this point that Borg's Jesus research reveals its gnostic impulse. Borg sifts through the evidence of the Gospels and emerges with a Jesus the jury would like, with a Jesus more in tune with today's new spirituality, Borg's own spirituality, and gnostic spirituality than with the ancient Palestinian world. The "historical" Jesus that Borg identifies (and therefore, partially presumes) is, at root, a strangely ahistorical figure, and nowhere is this more apparent than in this issue of eschatology. The weight of current New Testament scholarship sees Jesus as a Galilean Jew who held to the beliefs and observed the customs of first-century Judaism and who furthermore was in some way related to the particular form of eschatological Judaism found in the John the Baptist movement. This would tend to underscore the notion that Jesus was himself a thoroughgoing eschatological Jew. There is simply no way to imagine John the Baptist, Jesus' mentor, other than as an eschatological prophet. Borg evidently assumes, then, that Jesus split with John on this critical point and became somehow noneschatological, or even antieschatological. Even Jesus couldn't fully break the pattern though, so the early church and the New Testament writers apparently slipped back into that Jewish eschatological stuff and even revised the scripts to put this view into Jesus' mouth. If so, Borg shares this view with his colleagues in the Jesus Seminar, and commenting on this, Hays says,

> The depiction of Jesus as a Cynic philosopher with no concern about Israel's destiny, no connection with the concerns and hopes that animated his Jewish contemporaries, no interest in the interpretation of scripture, and no message of God's coming eschatological judgment is quite simply—an ahistorical fiction, achieved by the surgical removal of Jesus from his Jewish context. . . . One would have thought that the tragic events of our century might have warned us to be wary of biblical scholars who deny the Jewishness of Jesus.[68]

Borg, no doubt aware that one of the criticisms of the Jesus Seminar is that it is tinged with an anti-Semitic bias, makes sure he affirms the Jewishness of Jesus. "Jesus was deeply Jewish," he says. "He spoke as a Jew to other Jews."[69] Borg is at pains to talk about the many ways that Jesus is connected to his Jewish culture, faith, and practice.

But what belies this talk of a Jewish Jesus is the Jesus who actually shows up at the end of Borg's historical detective work. Who is this "historical" Jesus? He grew up as a boy in small-town Galilee, participating in the common practices of his religion, Judaism. But at some point he became a "religious seeker," embarked on a "religious quest," and had a "conversion experience" in which religious impulses and energies became central to his life. This led to his adult role as a "spirit person," just "one of many mediators of the sacred," one of a class of people who have "a strong sense of there being more to reality than the tangible world of our ordinary experience." He was also a teacher of wisdom and a social prophet who turned a withering critique on the Jewish social world, particularly its view of the purity system, and on the "domination system" of the empire. He had remarkable verbal gifts and "was clearly exceptionally intelligent." He was "both a right brain and left brain thinker," was courageous, and had a magnetic and compelling personal presence, and we can even imagine him "going to the theater as a young man." While it would be anachronistic to call him a "feminist," he nevertheless had feminist instincts and formed a community of "equals" embodying an "egalitarian praxis."[70]

Funny, he doesn't *look* Jewish. This mystical, egalitarian, left brain–right brain, intellectually keen, theater-going, politically leftish Jesus looks less like a Galilean Jewish peasant and more like someone you would run into in the faculty club at the university. In fact, come to think of it, this small-town boy who left home on a religious quest and had a mystical conversion experience on the way to becoming a bright and personable sage and social critic, especially taking on rigid religion and political oppression, looks a lot like Borg.

And that is no coincidence. As New Testament scholar Ulrich Luz once remarked, "It is amazing what can be surmised with a hypothetically reconstructed Jesus text!"[71] I do not challenge Borg's knowledge or his competence as a Jesus historian. I am not a New Testament scholar myself, and I yield that territory to Borg and others. I am simply pointing out what other biblical scholars have observed: that attempting to reconstruct the historical Jesus has almost inevitably led to self-projection. More than a century ago Martin Kähler noted that people who try to draw out of the four Gospels a biography of Jesus are compelled to insert into the process a "fifth Gospel," namely their own faith and priorities.[72] Jesus historians start out gazing into the Gospels, but the written texts quickly turn into mirrors reflecting the needs, issues, and faces of the scholars themselves. As George Tyrell once said of Adolf von Harnack's attempt to describe the life and message of the historical Jesus, "The Christ that Harnack sees, looking back through nineteen centuries of Catholic darkness, is only the reflection of a Liberal Protestant face, seen at the bottom of a deep well."[73] Trying to strip away post-Easter descriptions of Jesus in the New Testament does not leave standing the "real" Jesus; it leaves instead, as Dunn says, "an empty stage waiting to be filled by some creative amalgam of the historian's own imagination and values."

Paul Ricoeur agrees that the quest for the "historical Jesus" always turns back on itself to reveal more about the searcher than about Jesus:

> [A]re we not setting ourselves the impossible task of reconstructing a "life of Jesus"? Has not the history of redaction and form criticism shown us that this understanding has already failed and that it had to fail? Liberal theology, underestimating the strictly exegetical obstacles to this enterprise, sought to treat the christological inter-pretations as an added-on superstructure that could be removed so that one could write a life of Jesus freed of every dogmatic and eccle-siological prejudice. However, as Albert Schweitzer demonstrated in his history of these lives of Jesus, in the final analysis each one reflected the historian's own vision of the world or that of his epoch, and so each was therefore paradoxically revealed to be just as theo-logically motivated as were the narratives it sought to replace.[74]

Indeed, Borg's picture of Jesus is not the result of a careful piecing together of "neutral" historical data but a portrait painted in the colors of Borg's own theological palette. I believe that the "historical" Jesus we meet in the pages of Borg's writing lacks both the specificity of an eth-nic Jew and the eschatological urgency of the Judaism of his day, not because Borg has one ounce of anti-Semitism, but rather because Borg has a pound of the gnostic impulse. Borg has in his own faith the gnos-tic emphasis on present spiritual reality rather than eschatological hope. Small wonder that the detective sifts the evidence, analyzes the clues, and points the finger at a Jesus whose faith and commitments are strik-ingly like his own.

PREACHING TO NEO-GNOSTICS

Why care about all of this? Why care about the minutiae of Borg's thought? He is a gentle and generous man who seeks the good of the church, and he is not in the least the enemy. I do not relish engaging him in debate (in fact, I imagine he would have much to say back to me). Yes, he both represents and feeds a new gnosticism in the church; but why get worked up over that? What difference does it make that in the pews of many congregations are bright, inquisitive gnostics? Why should it concern us that there are good and loyal church folk out there who believe their souls to be immortal sparks of the divine, that God is to be found by searching within, that while most Christians have a rule-bound, doctrine-based brand of Christianity, the true faith for the enlightened is to break free from all that, that spirituality is the goal, that the resurrection was not about Jesus' body but was a moment of spiritual illumination for the followers of Jesus then and now? Why not let them be? Why not see them as simply representatives of alternative forms of Christianity?

Perhaps Bart Ehrman is right when he says that there is now a new-found and more tolerant "sense that alternative understandings of Christianity from the past [including gnosticism] can be cherished yet today, that they can provide insights even now for those of us who are concerned about the world and our place in it."[75] The church at its best has always celebrated free and courageous inquiry about its doctrinal claims. The gnostic agenda has merit. We do need a spiritual rebirth, a maturity of faith that moves beyond childish and uninformed views of Jesus, sin, church, Bible, and eschatological expectations. We do need a recovery of the wisdom tradition in our faith. Why not welcome the new gnosticism instead of fretting over it?

The answer is in the great commandment. "You shall love the Lord your God with all your heart and mind and soul, and your neighbor as yourself." To search only, or even mainly, for "the God within" is finally a failure of love. It is first of all a failure to love the God of Abraham and Sarah, Isaac and Jacob, and Rachel and Deborah, Jesus and Paul, Priscilla and Aquila: the God who created the world by his word, the God who parted the Red Sea and delivered Israel from slavery, the God who was at work in Jesus of Nazareth and raised him from the dead, the God who encountered Saul on the Damascus road, the God who sustained and empowers the Christian community to be bold in mission to the world. To love God with our minds and hearts and souls means loving the God who surely speaks to the quiet places of our hearts, but who also stands outside of us, loving us with a fierce and demanding love, never letting us go, even when our hearts are prone to wander. The "God within" almost never sends prophets to stir us up or turn over tables in our temples.

But gnosticism is also finally a failure truly to love the neighbor. Certainly there is plenty of talk among the new gnostics about having a "heart and a passion for justice," because God is passionate for justice. But it hangs in midair, and there is little to sustain such heartfelt passion. The panentheistic, nonacting God of "Is-ness" may really care about justice, and wise, right-thinking, enlightened adherents of this God may share this God-consciousness, but that is quite a different thing from saying that the God of Jesus Christ is acting in the world to restore the goodness of creation and that we are called as the people of God to be a part of that divine action by loving and serving our neighbors. A Christ whose resurrection occurs only in our minds has no right to call us to put our bodies on the line for justice. But a risen Christ whose body still bears the marks of the wounds will send Christians passionately, even joyfully, marching across the bridge at Selma, hammering shingles on Habitat for Humanity houses, and changing bedpans in an AIDS hospice.

When all of the strands are bundled together, gnosticism doesn't merely inflect the accent of the Christian faith; it changes its grammar, distorts its memory, and makes it speak in a tongue alien to the gospel. It transforms the sacraments and practices of the faith from the embodied expression of the life-giving cry "Emmanuel! God is with us!" into churchy and finally dispensable external forms of an immaterial and truer spiritual reality. It replaces our commitment to a God who acts in history, who saves us even from ourselves, who gives us hope, and who promises to bring the tragic story of humanity to consummation by making Christ all-in-all, with a timeless, ahistorical gnosis that makes us even more self-absorbed and narcissistic than we already are.

Preaching to neo-gnostics is not easy. It is not as if they are innocent children waiting to be taught. No, they *know* stuff; in fact they celebrate the fact that they know stuff, because their knowing forms a firewall between themselves and those they fear the most—the naive believer, the fundamentalist know-nothing, and the judgmental religious parent. The gnostic impulse calls forth two responses from the preacher. First, the preacher needs to realize that preaching in our milieu is now a form of interfaith dialogue. The old gods have come back in our culture to reclaim their devotees, among them the god of gnosis. The gnostic impulse is not without its virtues, rewards, and satisfactions, and the preacher must be willing to recognize, name, and even rejoice in them. "Athenians, I see how extremely religious you are in every way," Paul began his sermon on the Areopagus, both connecting with his cultured audience and tilling the soil to plant among them the gospel seed.

Second, preaching must now move beyond the gentle stories and the warm pastoral encouragements and take up the harder and more meticulous work of challenging the shallow spiritualities of our time—

"What you therefore worship as unknown," Paul said, "this I proclaim to you" (Acts 17:23)—and teaching the grammar of the gospel. It is easy for today's gnostics to reject the doctrines of the incarnation, providence, and eschatology as intellectually bankrupt and meaningless when they have never heard them proclaimed with intelligence and passion. It is easy for today's gnostics to scoff at the idea of an empty tomb or the resurrection of the body when the only category they have for imagining them is as some crude supernatural magic show. It is easy for today's gnostics to charge that traditional Christianity has nothing meaningful to say to the question of how God could be loving and powerful in a world of terrible evil when no preacher in their hearing has ever wrestled with that issue.

Christian doctrine seems, to many of today's spiritual seekers, to be so much unnecessary baggage, ten impossible things to believe before breakfast. What we preachers need to do is to stop leaving Christian doctrine on the seminary cutting-room floor, to stop buying into the gnostic notion that faith is simply undifferentiated spiritual experience, to take the theological plunge, and to reclaim our role as pulpit teachers of the Christian faith. When the second-century bishop Irenaeus faced a mushrooming gnosticism in his own parish and culture, his genius, as Luke Johnson has described it, was to recognize that a threefold response was needed:

> He countered the claim of esoteric teachings with the public rule of faith. He countered the claim of secret gospels with the writings read public in the assembly, the canon of Scripture (Old Testament as well as New). He countered the claim of private teacher/revealers with the public tradition of bishops extending from the apostles to his own day.[76]

To put these strategies into play in our own content would mean that we would, with as much gentleness and hospitality as possible, publicly teach and preach the great themes, ideas, and claims of the Christian faith, embody in our preaching the discovery and delight of the scripture, and show why the church sees it as a matter of human flourishing to preserve the contours and claims of the gospel. As theologian Christopher Morse has said, "To believe in God is not to believe everything. In fact, it is hard to imagine what believing everything would mean. . . . Surely a tendency to trust everything without awareness of what is untrustworthy is not the faith in God to which we have been called by the gospel."[77]

We need to unpack the truth claims of the gospel and to teach the inner dynamics and connections of the Christian gospel, particularly in those very places where gnosticism poses its strongest challenge. For example, we need to show, in instruction and story, in example and poetic expression, that when Christians put their bodies on the line for others—whether this takes the form of Martin Luther King Jr. showing up at a garbage strike in Memphis, or a middle-aged guy forgoing a Saturday of golf in order to work in a soup kitchen, or Albert Schweitzer founding a hospital in West Africa, or a mother getting out of bed at night to comfort her sick and frightened child—this is not just because Jesus inspires us to be good to others; these "body acts" are a speaking forth with the language of our real bodies the grammar implied in the incarnation of Jesus Christ and the embodiment of hope inscribed in his resurrection. We need to help congregations move beyond finger-wagging, psychic guilt-inducing notions of sin and toward a biblical understanding of sin as the tragic dimension of human existence. And we need to preach the eschatological hope that reverberates throughout the gospel. As perhaps something of a test case, in the next chapter we will explore the travails and the challenges of preaching the contested doctrine of eschatology.

5

Preaching in the Future-Perfect Tense: Eschatology and Proclamation

There is a time of the night between midnight and dawn when people despair.

—Anatole Broyard, *Intoxicated by My Illness*[1]

The comedian George Carlin, in one of his marvelous standup routines, expressed astonishment over those opinion polls on television networks like CNN and Fox, where some debatable question is posed and people are invited to phone in and vote their views. "Did you ever notice," Carlin said, "there's always, like, 18 percent who vote 'I don't know'? It costs a dollar to make those calls," Carlin said, "and they're voting 'I don't know.'" Carlin imagined some guy seeing the question of the day on the TV screen and saying to his wife, "Honey, give me that phone!" He shouts "I don't know!" into the phone and then says proudly to his wife, "Sometimes you have to stand up for what you believe you're not sure about." Carlin went on to speculate that these same people probably call 1-900 numbers for $3.00 a minute to say, "I'm not in the mood."

Suppose, however, that there were a preacher's version of these phone polls, and the question of the day was "What do you think about eschatology? What are your views on the specific shape and character of Christian hope for the future? What do you make of the New Testament's promise that 'the Son of Man will come in the clouds with great power and glory'?" Most preachers would probably vote "I don't know." And as for actually preaching a sermon on the theme of eschatology? "Well . . . I'm not in the mood."

111

THE LOSS OF ESCHATOLOGY IN PREACHING

How today's mainstream pulpit grew silent about eschatology, about the classic "last things," is a complex story, but it is also a remarkable story, because those of us who preach today are the heirs of preachers in a not-too-distant past who spoke often, clearly, and confidently of the Christian hope for people and for all of creation. For example, the children of nineteenth-century Presbyterian clergyman Lyman Beecher remembered vividly that he prayed every day, "Overturn and overturn till He whose right it is shall come and reign, King of nations and King of saints."[2] Among educated clergy in the churches we have come to call "mainline," the language of heaven, hell, Christ's coming reign, and the final judgment were recurring and important topics of sermons in the nineteenth century, but by the close of the twentieth century a veil of embarrassment had been thrown over the whole matter. Preachers in 1850 spoke eloquently and frequently about the consummation of history in the return of Jesus Christ and of the pilgrimage of the soul toward eternal life, but they would have blushed at the mention of sex. Today many preachers are willing to discuss life's fleshier problems with the frankness of Jerry Springer, but the prospect of preaching a sermon on the second coming or judgment day chills the blood.

A number of years ago, a reader of the official denominational magazine of the United Church of Christ and the United Presbyterian Church sent this no-doubt earnest query to the question-answer column:

> Q. Why are there so few sermons in our churches on the Second Coming? Is this part of our belief or not?

The wise "answer person" replied this way:

> A. Not all Christians think alike on matters of theology, but it would be hard for someone to feel at home in our tradition who did not understand God as the One who has come, who is present . . . in our lives today, *and* who is yet to come in whatever form the future ends up taking. To literalize the Second Coming is to ruin both its beauty and its significance. To ignore it is to avoid what may be the most important part of the Gospel we know about, since the past and present, relatively speaking, are brief, while tomorrow borders on forever.[3]

In a later issue of the magazine, another reader reacted to this answer:

I compliment the Rev._____ for his illusive non-answer to what I am sure was a serious question concerning the Second Coming of Jesus Christ. If I understood his answer, he said, in effect, "We don't all agree. But if you want to be comfortable in the UCC/UPC, you will need to agree that Jesus is coming again, but not really—for if you actually believe in the Second Coming you will ruin both its beauty and its significance. Yet you can't ignore it because it is in the future."[4]

Like this later correspondent, we may wince at the confused gobbledygook of the editor's answer to the original question, but most of us recognize in ourselves the same tendency to sand down the jagged, offending surfaces of eschatology. I am, myself, contemptuous of the naive literalism underlying, say, the *Left Behind* series of books, and when I think about it longer, deeply concerned about the political blood root that sometimes grows in that neglected back lot of the biblical garden. But whenever more mainstream preachers actually enter the apocalyptic and eschatological territories of the Bible, we suddenly become disoriented tourists who don't know the language, who stumble over the customs, who are made queasy by the diet, and who can't find our way back to the hotel. What do you think about eschatology? I don't know. What about a sermon on the last things? I'm not in the mood.

What has happened to American preaching in the last one hundred years to cause the trumpet to lose its certain sound on eschatology? The story, as I read it, is that our nineteenth-century forebears—Presbyterian, Congregationalist, Methodist, Episcopal, Baptist, and other clergy in the American Protestant mainstream (mostly in the North)—married themselves to a form of eschatological thinking that was so fragile and intellectually untenable that when it collapsed under its own weight, so great was its ruin that almost nothing could be salvaged. This view of eschatology was finally conflicted internally, ham-handed in terms of biblical hermeneutics, and notably ill equipped to withstand the hurricane winds of social and intellectual change that swept over the American religious landscape in the late nineteenth and early twentieth centuries. We are still walking around, stunned, in the dust and ash of its collapse.

American church historian James Moorhead has persuasively described how a wide swath of educated clergy in the mid-nineteenth century held firmly to a version of eschatology known as postmillennialism. Although there were various strains of the postmillennial view, essentially postmillennialism affirmed the role of the Christian church, working for progress and enlightenment in society, gradually effecting the kingdom and its purposes in human affairs. After the church had labored for Christ for a "millennium," which was taken to be not an exact period of time but rather a symbol for a long season of churchly work and progress, Christ would come again to reign in victory over his kingdom. This view of the course and consummation of history was actually a rather ingenious attempt to combine stout loyalty to the Bible, on the one hand, with an equally strong and optimistic commitment to social gradualism, on the other,[5] and it was described by a contemporary as "the commonly received opinion" of the day.[6] But this was a marriage of biblical interpretation and social theory that was doomed from the beginning.

From the biblical side came an apocalyptic view of time, complete with the full pyrotechnics of trumpet-blowing angels, howling winds, stars falling from the heavens, "the Son of Man coming in clouds with great power and glory," and all the nations gathered before the throne to be divided into the sheep and the goats. Their strict, mostly literal view of the Bible forced postmillennialists to take with utmost seriousness all of the biblical images of the second coming, of the ultimate cataclysmic denouement of history, and of death as the personal moment of standing in the breach between heaven and hell. Make no mistake about it, postmillennialists believed that one day "this old world was gonna reel and rock," and their brand of eschatology had, as Moorhead says, a "hard residue of apocalypticism."[7]

On the other side, though, these clergy were informed modern people, sort of streetwise Hegelians, and from the social and philosophical zeitgeist they drew an evolutionary view of history, moving ever onward up the ramp of progress. Postmillennialists were thoughtful denizens of their age who drank freely and deeply from the wells of developmental philosophy. History may be moving toward an omega point, they thought, but it was not blindly stumbling toward Armageddon. History was, rather, unfolding, evolving, and progressing toward the time when Christ would be all in all, and human beings had a role to play in this grand redevelopment project.

Now how does one hold together apocalypticism, on the one hand, and developmentalism, on the other? Well, remember the postmillennialists were, after all, *post*-millennial. The shaking of the world's foundations was surely coming, but not yet, not soon. These events would occur only after a millennium of social and moral progress, an extensive span of time in which Christ and his people were at work in the world gradually nurturing and developing society toward the ultimate kingdom. "[T]his was an effort," Moorhead says, "to maintain a sense of the End while keeping it at a seemly distance."[8]

We have to admire their achievement. Apocalypticism and social developmentalism are odd bedfellows to be sure, and only the most heroic expenditure of energy and intellectual capital could keep their relationship from ending up in divorce court. As biblical scholar John Barton has noted, apocalyptic poetry and historical prose are usually not commensurate. When scripture says, "The stars will fall from heaven and the sun will cease its shining; the moon will be turned to blood and fire mingled with hail will fall from the heavens," we don't expect the next phrase to be, "The rest of the country will be partly cloudy with scattered showers."[9]

But part of what made people happy and satisfied to be postmillennialists is that it generated a kinder and gentler eschatology than the alternative: premillennialism. Premillennialists, who barked their fearful theology mainly from the fringes, held to a Halloween-nightmare view of the end of time. Human history was a soiled failure of sinful rebellion, and a Christ with wrathful, burning eyes was coming with his terrible swift sword at any minute to clean house and rescue his tiny righteous remnant. Mainstream Protestants, however, were far more relaxed. They had 1,000 years, a whole millennium, to do what Protestants do best: toil like worker bees Christianizing the nation, evangelizing the world, improving society, and otherwise socially engineering countless institutions efficiently after the pattern of Christ. The grandchildren of premillennialists are putting signs beside Alabama freeways warning, "Are you ready? Christ is coming soon!" while the grandchildren of postmillennialists are running church bureaucracies and capital campaigns.

What the confident and socially suave postmillennialists did not know, though, was that—like the *Titanic*, another nineteenth-century concept pushed into the dangerous seas of the twentieth-century—postmillennialism was headed for an iceberg. To summon another metaphor, postmillennialism rested uneasily on a three-legged stool. The first leg was a naive view of the Bible as literally and factually accurate. The second leg was the idea that Christianity was a religion so unlike, so superior to other religions as to constitute a difference not just in degree but in kind. Christianity was the unique revelation of God, and all other religions were but ignorant paganisms doomed to be superseded and left in

Christianity's evolutionary wake. The third leg was a proud view of human beings as superior rational and moral beings, higher than and separate from the rest of creation, and thus capable of engineering the kingdom's arrival.

What happened to this three-legged stool? To put it in shorthand, German higher criticism and science sawed off the first leg, biblical literalism; anthropology and the comparative study of religions sawed off the second (for example, Andrew Dickson White, the president of Cornell, reported that he lost his faith in the miracle stories of the New Testament when he discovered in the 1850s that Islamic beliefs included claims of the same sorts of miracles[10]); and Darwin and later Freud sawed off the third leg.

As a result, the predominant eschatology of American religion, all of its supports compromised, collapsed in a heap. When it fell, it fell hard. Unitarian Oliver Wendell Holmes's famous poem "The Deacon's Masterpiece, or the Wonderful One-Hoss Shay," which poked fun at tightly constructed Puritan theology by describing a carriage where every part was logically crafted and each piece just a strong as the next one, could just as well have described the fall of postmillennial theology:

> You see, of course, if you're not a dunce,
> How it went to pieces all at once,
> All at once, and nothing first,
> Just as bubbles do when they burst.
> End of the wonderful one-hoss shay.
> Logic is logic. That's all I say.

Early in the twentieth century, the essayist Edmund Gosse spoke for a whole generation when he remembered the very moment when he lost his eschatological virginity, when his childhood faith in a future, coming Christ evaporated into thin air. He was a schoolboy, standing alone in the school yard, and suddenly the air around him grew still. "There was," he wrote,

> an absolute silence below and around me, a magic of suspense seemed to keep every topmost twig from waving. Over my soul there swept an immense wave of emotion. Now, surely now, the great final change must be approaching. I gazed up into the tenderly-colored sky, and I broke irresistibly into speech. "Come now, Lord Jesus," I cried. . . . I waited awhile, watching. . . . Then a little breeze sprang up and the branches danced. . . . From far below there rose to me

the chatter of boys returning home. The tea bell rang. . . . "The Lord has not come, the Lord will never come," I muttered, and in my heart the artificial edifice of extravagant faith began to totter and crack.[11]

Essentially within the span of a single generation, the reigning eschatological view of American mainstream Christianity fell to pieces. As Ernst Troeltsch stated just before World War I, "The eschatological bureau is closed these days."[12] And the mainstream pulpit grew strangely silent about the "final things."

THE RETURN OF THE REPRESSED

The French cultural critic Andre Malraux once observed that the figure of Christ, once so prominent as a theme in classical Western art, had largely disappeared in modern art. But Christ, Malraux claimed, was not really gone. Instead of being the subject of paintings, Christ, under other names, had become absorbed as the inner principle of modern art.[13]

Just so, eschatology, once a major motif in American theology and preaching, did not really disappear. Rather it reappeared in the morphed form of confidence in the doctrine of progress, confidence in human powers to transform society in the present tense. The language of an eschatological future, now turned to vapor, was sucked up into the engine of the optimistic present tense, and mainstream American preachers, deprived of eschatological language, devoid of a future hope, became instead apostles of progress in its many forms—moral progress, social improvement, the "power of positive thinking," church growth, and the psychotherapeutic gospel. Even the growing agnosticism and atheism of late nineteenth- and early twentieth-century America was, in the final analysis, mostly Christian eschatology transformed into a domesticated and intellectually acceptable doctrine of progress. "Progress did for unbelievers," claims historian James Turner,

> what God did for believers. The existence of God assured believers that the universe had a purpose. An agnostic had to conclude that the final purpose, if any, of the cosmos eluded human knowledge. But one could still feel that one's own strivings did not evaporate into nothingness, that they held an infinitesimal but salient place in the pilgrimage of the race.[14]

Woody Allen once composed a satirical Greek drama. In the final act of this play, when the human race was embroiled in conflict and hopeless problems, the script called for the god Zeus, thunderbolts extruding from his hands, to be lowered onto the stage to straighten out all human dilemmas—deus ex machina. Unfortunately, though, as Zeus is being lowered to the stage, something goes wrong with the harness and a wire wraps around Zeus's neck and strangles him. The stunned actors look at each other for a moment, and then one of them says, "God is dead. Ad lib the ending."[15]

The main problem with progress as a replacement for eschatology, of course, is that for all of its brave talk of transformation, we are basically condemned to the possibilities already inherent in the human prospect. It is finally a form of pragmatic atheism; God is dead. Ad lib the ending. When the church and its preachers become apostles of progress, in its various forms, we unwittingly become enemies of the faith. As James Turner has noted about the nineteenth century, it was not the enemies of God who most damaged the faith; it was the "get right with modernity" friends of God who did God in:

> [R]eligion caused unbelief. In trying to adapt their religious beliefs to socioeconomic change, to new moral challenges, to novel problems of knowledge, to the tightening standards of science, the defenders of God slowly strangled Him. If anyone is to be arraigned for deicide, it is not Charles Darwin but his adversary Bishop Samuel Wilberforce; not the godless Robert Ingersoll but the godly Beecher family.[16]

In our own day, both on the left and on the right, there continues the sucking up of eschatological hope into the energies of present-tense optimism and progress. Listen once again to the words of this popular hymn, generated in the Roman Catholic world, but finding traction among progressive Protestants too:

> Not in the dark of buildings confining,
>   not in some heaven, light years away—
> but here in this place the new light is shining;
>   now is the kingdom, now is the day!
>
> Gather us in and hold us forever;
>   gather us in and make us your own;
> gather us in, all peoples together,
>   fire of love in our flesh and our bone![17]

"Not in the dark of buildings confining" is the anti-institutional, antiembodiment, gnostic prejudice of the reigning "I'm spiritual, but not religious" popular piety, and "not in some heaven, light years away" is the accompanying rejection of the future tense as a meaningful register for religious experience. Since, in the view of this hymn, the symbol of heaven can only be a relic of a now dead, naive literalism or a piece of world-denying, pie-in-the sky irrelevance, everything meaningful gets lodged in the mystical, disembodied present tense. We beat John Lennon to the punch in imagining "there's no heaven."

Or as we have already noted, theologian Marcus Borg claims that "Jesus himself seems to have believed in an afterlife, but he doesn't talk about it very much."[18] Borg goes on to say, "Put most simply, salvation means to be saved from our predicament . . . [a] multilayered transformation of our lives in this world,"[19] and again, "[t]he biblical understandings of salvation are focused on this world, not the next."[20]

Biblical scholar J. Christiaan Beker puts it well when, in assessing the continuing value of Paul's apocalyptic and eschatological thought for today, he points out that claims like Borg's—that "biblical understandings of salvation are focused on this world, not the next"—imply a false and unbiblical dichotomy:

> God's act in Christ focuses our attention on the present time as an "apocalyptic" time, that is, on the either-or of our allegiance: do we either serve Christ or the powers of this world? The apocalyptic categories of Paul's gospel focus primarily on the "now" of our decision, but they do so only because of the motivating and beckoning power of God's final triumph. For the "now" of our decision is only then realistic when it is inspired by the vision of God's kingdom. Without that apocalyptic vision, our hope becomes either a romantic illusion or a constrictive demand because it collapses God's coming triumph in our present personal stance and will power.[21]

As for the theological right, the big news is that even the evangelical world, almost the last segment to hold onto eschatological claims, usually in premillenial form, has suffered, a century later, the same collapse of eschatology as mainstream Christians. Evangelical preachers, like their mainstream counterparts, have become evangelists, not for the God who breaks in from the future, but instead for progress, and their sermons too have moved into the present-tense genre of Wisdom literature. Consider Rick Warren, the Hawaiian-shirted preacher to an SUV-driving congregation at California's Saddleback Church and the author of *The Purpose-Driven Life*. Among his sermons on healing hidden wounds, finding the courage to make a difference, and the essentials of life, Rick Warren will throw in an occasional sermon on heaven and the afterlife, but you get the sense his heart isn't in it. As for Joel Osteen, the pastor of Houston's gargantuan Lakewood megachurch, his focus is firmly on personal progress in the present tense. What is the Christian faith about if it isn't about *Your Best Life Now*?

Ironically, right at the time that the pulpit has become silent on matters eschatological, contemporary systematic theology is marked by a remarkable resurgence of eschatological thinking. The interest in eschatology is not confined to systematics. In novels and movies and popular songs, eschatological themes are pressing forward. I think especially of recent novels with eschatological themes: Oscar Hijuelos's *Mr. Ives' Christmas,* Leif Enger's *Peace Like a River,* and Cormac McCarthy's *The Road* and *No Country for Old Men.* In this last novel, Ed Tom Bell is an aging Texas county sheriff investigating a desert drug deal gone terribly wrong that resulted in several brutal deaths and the disappearance of a couple of million dollars of cash. Spinning forward from this crime, two plots unfold simultaneously in the novel, only to converge at the end. In the first, Bell and his deputy investigate the crime, while in the second, Anton Chigurh, a cold-blooded hit man hired by the drug lords, ruthlessly tracks down the missing cash.

As the novel proceeds, Bell and Chigurh begin to assume symbolic and theological status. Bell is a Pauline figure, a man who used to trust the law, but now, overwhelmed by the power of evil in the world, knows that the law cannot save him or society. He has begun to realize that, as a lawman, he is fighting not just crime, flesh, and blood, but the powers and principalities. He says,

> I think if you were Satan and you were just settin around tryin to think up somethin that would just bring the human race to its knees what you would probably come up with is narcotics. Maybe he did. I told that to somebody at breakfast the other mornin and they asked me if I believed in Satan. . . . I had to think about that. I guess as a boy I did. Come the middle years my belief I reckon had waned somewhat. Now I'm startin to lean back the other way.[22]

Late in the novel, he muses about why he went into law enforcement in the first place: "Part of it was I always thought I could at least someway put things right and I guess I just don't feel that way no more. . . .

I'm being asked to stand for somethin that I don't have the same belief in it I once did."[23] Bell reflects to himself about the only hope he can imagine, a hungering for redemption that transcends the powers of humanity, "I wake up sometimes way in the night and I know as certain as death that there aint nothing short of the second comin of Christ that can slow this train."

Chigurh, on the other hand, is the embodiment of random, chaotic, meaningless evil. He kills at a whim, and without remorse. In one terrible scene, he is about to kill a young woman who is utterly innocent, no threat to him, and her murder is a completely unnecessary act of pure evil. Cruelly, having told her that he plans to kill her, he pretends to give her a chance to live by taking out a coin and asking her to call a toss, heads or tails. "God would not want me to do that," she replies. Chigurh then, as a last word before he shoots her, mocks any fleeting hope the coin-toss gesture may have stirred in the woman: "I thought it not too much to ask," he says to her, "that you have a final glimpse of hope in the world to lift your heart before the shroud drops, the darkness. Do you see?"

"Oh God," she says, "Oh God."

As a typical law-and-order story, *No Country for Old Men* is a tragedy. It ends with Chigurh still roaming the earth and all the good people either dead or defeated. It is a story of gloom and loss. But on the very last page of the novel, Bell, now retired from his job as sheriff, gives way to his memories. He first remembers, with amazement, an old house he once saw with a stone water trough, hewn from solid rock, which had been there for over a hundred years. He thinks about the man who chiseled that stone trough, working maybe an hour or two each evening after dinner, fashioning something that would be around for a thousand years, long after the house was gone. He wonders why a man would do that. "And I have to say that the only thing I can think is that there was some sort of promise in his heart. . . . I would like to be able to make that kind of promise."[24]

He then remembers two dreams he had about his deceased father, who was also a sheriff in his day, an old-fashioned man of unbending integrity:

> I don't remember the first one all that well but it was about meetin him in town somewheres and he give me some money and I think I lost it. But the second one, it was like we was both back in older times and I was on horseback goin through the mountains of a

night. Goin through this pass in the mountains. It was cold and there was snow on the ground and he rode past me and kept on goin. Never said nothin. He just rode on past and he had his blanket wrapped around him and he had his head down and when he rode past I seen he was carryin fire in a horn the way people used to do and I could see the horn from the light inside of it. About the color of the moon. And in the dream I knew that he was goin on ahead and he was fixin to make a fire somewhere out there in all that dark and all that cold and I knew that whenever I got there he would be there. And then I woke up.[25]

This is a surprising eschatological reflection. Almost nothing in the novel prepares us for it, but, in retrospect, everything has been leaning toward it. Understood theologically, it signals that hope lies in the God who goes ahead of us, "to make a fire somewhere out there" in all the dark and cold. But this is no pie-in-the-sky promise; it is the kind of promise that in a transient and broken world can set you to work with a hammer and chisel, working on something that will be around when all that decays has taken its toll.

In the film version of *No Country for Old Men*, this eschatological speech is the last scene. When Bell has finished speaking these words, the credits roll. At most showings, audiences sit puzzled, unsure what to make of this curious ending. In one movie house, it was reported that when the screen went to black, a man in the theater shouted into the darkness, "What the &^%$% was *that* all about!" With the eschatological voice gone silent in our culture, the language of promise, the language of a redemption beyond human striving, strikes uncomprehending ears.

Another recent eschatological film is *The Shawshank Redemption*, a movie also full of life's despair, a story set in a dreary and cruel prison. In one scene, as an act of defiance, one of the prisoners locks himself in the room where the public address system for the prison is located and puts on loudspeakers all over the prison a duet from Mozart's *The Marriage of Figaro*. This music is heard not just as Mozart, but as music from another world. One of the inmates says,

> I have no idea to this day what those two Italian ladies were singin' about. . . . I like to think they were singin' about something so beautiful it can't be expressed in words, and makes your heart ache because of it. I tell you those voices soared, higher and farther than anybody in a gray place dares to dream. It was like some beautiful

bird flapped into our drab little cage and made these walls dissolve away . . . and for the briefest of moments, every last man at Shawshank felt free.[26]

That too is an eschatological parable. Our novelists and artists are sensing the power in the eschatological vision. So far, though, this renewal of eschatological thinking and language has bypassed the American pulpit, which remains stuck in the funeral rites of the death of nineteenth-century thought forms.

Vibrant Christian preaching depends upon the recovery of its eschatological voice, an eschatology that avoids literalism while insisting that the full disclosure of God is not fully contained in the present tense. As Duke Ellington once said, "There are two types of music, good and bad, and you can tell them apart by listening." Just so, there are two types of eschatology, and you can tell them apart by living them out. The first kind of eschatology depends upon a literalistic grip on biblical images and results in a gospel that is intellectually implausible, stuck in the clouds of a pious and irrelevant heaven that never touches earth. If that is our only option, the retreat into a self-contained present tense is our only ethical choice. The second kind of eschatology, however, allows the eschatological affirmations that "Christ is risen!" and "Jesus is Lord!" to exercise tension upon the present tense, generating both judgment and promise, creating the possibility of ethical action in the world sustained by hope. "Perhaps the most important consequence of our exploration," writes Gayraud S. Wilmore in his book on eschatology, "will be the discovery that what Christians believe about the 'last things' may be first in terms of influence upon their behavior in the world."[27]

Some years ago I served on a committee called the Princeton University Chaplains' Advisory Council. We met only once a year, and our basic task was to hear reports from the chaplains on campus about their work. They would report, we would ask questions, and that was it. One year, we had heard the reports of the chaplains, and it was Q&A time. An older member of the council asked the chaplains, "What are the students like morally these days?" The chaplains looked at each other. Who wanted to answer that? Finally one of them, the Methodist chaplain, took a stab at it. "Well," she said, "I think you'd be pleased. They are pretty ambitious in terms of careers, but that's not all they are. A lot of them tutor kids after school. Some work in the night shelter and the soup kitchen for the homeless. Last week a group protested apartheid in South Africa. . . ." As she talked, the Jewish chaplain began to grin.

The more she talked, the bigger he grinned, until finally it became distracting. "Ed, am I saying something funny?" she said, slightly miffed. "No, no, I'm sorry," he replied. "I was just sitting here thinking. You are saying that the university students are good people, and you're right. And you're saying that they are involved in good social causes, and they are. But what I was thinking is that the one thing they lack is a vision of salvation." We all looked at the Jewish university chaplain. "No, it's true," he said. "If you don't have some vision of what God is doing to repair the whole creation, you can't get up every day and work in a soup kitchen. It finally beats you down."

As Karl Barth, commenting on Paul's claim in Romans 8:23 "for in hope we were saved," writes:

> The victory and fulfillment and presence of the Truth is ours only by hope. The Truth would not be Truth, if we, as we are, could apprehend it directly. How could the Truth be God, if it were for us but one possibility among others? How could we be saved by it, if it did not with compelling power urge us to hazard the leap into eternity, to dare to think what God thinks, to think freely, to think anew, to think wholly?
>
> . . . If Christianity be not thoroughgoing eschatology, there remains in it no relationship whatever with Christ. Spirit which does not at every moment point from death to the new life is not the Holy Spirit. . . . All that is not hope is wooden, hobbledehoy, blunt-edged and sharp-pointed, like the word 'Reality.' There there is no freedom, only imprisonment; no grace, but only condemnation and corruption; no divine guidance, only fate; no God, but only a mirror of unredeemed humanity.[28]

Barth goes on to say that "redemption is invisible, inaccessible, and impossible, for it meets us only in hope."[29] Yes, but the invisible becomes audible and the inaccessible is brought near in the "impossible possibility" of preaching. Like the risen Christ himself, preaching is a word from God's future embarrassingly and disturbingly thrust into the present, announcing the freedom in a time of captivity, the gift of peace to a world of conflict, and joy even as the lamenting continues. Preaching eschatologically, therefore, points not to unassailable evidence of God's reign, but to fleeting signs and wonders, ambiguous glimpses of what shall surely be already spring, like green shoots in the desert, a word from God's future that reshapes our imaginations. It is to speak from the end into the middle, to allow the word "It is finished" to liberate a world still very much in the making.

A student of mine told me that he spent a summer as a menial laborer on a construction crew. He said that his foreman was a person of kindness and grace. If a worker got sick on the job, he understood and made arrangements. If a worker had problems at home and was late or absent from work, he would cover for him. The one thing this foreman would not tolerate, though, was a worker who sat down on the job before the work was done. To sit down was a sign that the job was done, and to do so beforehand was a grievous violation of trust.

As the old creed says, "The third day he rose again from the dead; he ascended into heaven and sitteth on the right hand of God." To say that Jesus is "seated at the right hand of God" is essentially a claim that the work is done, that, in God's chronology, justice has been established and that, in God's eternal time, *shalom* even now reigns.

THE ESCHATOLOGICAL PULPIT

What, then, does eschatological preaching mean, what does it say, what does it sound like? We can name three characteristics of eschatological preaching.

1. First, to preach eschatologically is to participate in the promise that the fullness of God's *shalom* flows into the present, drawing it toward consummation. Eschatological preaching brings the finished work of God to bear on an unfinished world, summoning it to completion. Progress preaching tells people to gird up their loins and to use the resources at hand to make the world into a better place, and such preaching necessarily condemns people to failure and despair. Eschatological preaching promises a "new heaven and a new earth" and invites people to participate in a coming future that, while it is not dependent upon their success, is open to the labors of their hands.

A minister friend of mine in Atlanta at a downtown church planned one evening to go out to eat with his wife to celebrate their anniversary. His wife met him at the church, and the two of them headed out to the parking lot to take the car to the restaurant. But when they got outside they encountered a crisis. An elderly woman, a desperate look on her face, was kneeling on the sidewalk beside a man, her husband as it turns out, who was lying on his back in pain clutching his chest. My friend's wife ran quickly back into the church to call an ambulance, and my friend leaned over to comfort the man. "We have called for some help and they will be here soon . . . ," he began, but the man interrupted him.

"Charlie, forgive me," the man said.

"I'm not Charlie," my friend said. "My name is Sam." What Sam did not know until later is that Charlie was the man's son, and years before, the man had, in rage over something, disowned Charlie, and the two had not spoken in years.

The man looked up at Sam and reached out and touched his hand. "Charlie, please, forgive me."

"Just relax," Sam said. "Somebody will be here soon to get you to the hospital."

But the man suddenly clutched in terrible pain, and it was now clear that he would not make it to the hospital. With his last gasping energy he pulled on Sam's arm and begged, "Charlie, please, forgive me."

Sam followed his faithful instinct, reached out and put his hand on the man's forehead as a blessing and said, "I do forgive you. I do forgive you." Those were the last words the man ever heard in this life.

Later, when he learned what the circumstances were, Sam wondered if he had done the right thing. "I am not his son. The relationship was still broken. What right did I have to grant forgiveness?" Sam wondered. Then it came to him that his whole ministry was about this, that the whole Christian faith is about this. We have been given in Christ a restoration and a reconciliation that is already true, already whole, and we are beckoned from God's fullness to live into and toward what has already been given as a gift.

One thinks of the priest in Georges Bernanos's *Diary of a Country Priest*. Like all pastors, the priest knows the dark side of human life. He thinks about his congregation and he hears "the screaming of a beaten wife, the hiccup of a drunkard . . . poverty, lust." The priest says to himself, "No doubt I should turn from all this in disgust. And yet I feel that such distress, distress that has forgotten even its own name, that has ceased to reason or to hope, that lays its tortured head at random, will awaken one day on the shoulder of Jesus Christ."[30]

2. Second, eschatological preaching affirms that life under the providence of God has a shape, and that this shape is end-stressed; what happens in the middle is finally defined by the end. What is true about all narratives in the small sense is true of the gospel story in the largest sense: they reverse the flow of time. Everything is read from the end backwards, and events in the middle of things take their significance not just in themselves but in how they are related to the end. One of the best Christian expressions of this is the old African American spiritual, "Nobody knows who I am until Judgment Day." In the middle of

things, the forces of history may render a verdict on people. It may deem them to be chattel slaves, cannon fodder, or stubble for gas ovens. But history in the middle of things does not get to have the last word. God's eschatological fullness is the only truthfulness about who people really are. "Nobody knows who I am until Judgment Day."

In 1933 the lovely Bavarian village of Dachau became the site of an infamous Nazi concentration camp. Today, the barracks, crematoria, and other structures house a museum of the Holocaust and a memorial to its many victims. In the museum, there are photographs—unbelievably terrible photographs—of the reign of death and despair in Dachau and the other camps. One of these photographs shows a little girl—she must be about seven or eight—and her mother, being marched to the gas chamber at Auschwitz. The mother walks behind her daughter, powerless. There is nothing, absolutely nothing, she can do to stop what is about to happen. So, she commits the only act of love left to her; she places her hand over her daughter's eyes so the girl will not see where they are going.

I believe that every person who gazes at that photograph is moved to prayer. Secular or religious, all are provoked by that tragic scene to an anguished lament: "God, do not let this be the last word." There are, of course, responses to that cry that come from within history, from the resources available in the present: the camps were eventually liberated, a monument bearing the words "Never Again" in five languages stands at Dachau today, the display of the photograph of mother and daughter ensures that their suffering will be remembered and honored, commissions on the ending of genocide have been formed. But none of these things is a satisfactory response to the prayer, "God, do not let this be the last word."

Frank Kermode in his influential book *The Sense of an Ending* says that the basic structure of a plot is this: tick . . . tock. Tick gets the plot going, but everything leans forward and is governed by tock. Kermode says, "The Greeks . . . thought that even the gods could not change the past; but Christ did change it, rewrote it, and in a new way fulfilled it . . . the End changes all."[31]

I think this power of the tock, the power of the end to change everything, is the theological impact of the original ending of the Gospel of Mark. As you know, most scholars allow that the Gospel of Mark ends with 16:8—a figure robed in white announces the resurrection to the women at the tomb and tells them, "Go, tell his disciples and Peter that he is going ahead of you to Galilee; there you will see him." But the last line is "So they went out and fled from the tomb, for terror and amazement had seized them; and they said nothing to anyone, for they were afraid."

New Testament scholar Don Juel tells the story of a student of his who became fascinated by the Gospel of Mark and decided to memorize it and recite it orally in a public performance. This was no hastily contrived skit; the student prepared himself for several years, carefully studying the text, mapping the dramatic structure, grappling with the multiple characterizations, memorizing his lines.

The first performance was held in a large church, and the student, standing in front of the altar as he spoke, rendered a moving performance of Mark, bringing the Gospel to life. However, when he delivered that last line, "and they said nothing to anyone, for they were afraid," the audience sat there waiting in breathless anticipation, as if to say, "Yes. Go on, go on." The student, for all his preparation, had not completely thought this through. Unsettled by the audience's impatient gaze and unsure how to make a graceful exit, he shifted nervously from one foot to the other. Finally, after several seconds of awkward silence, he brightened and said, "Amen!" The relieved audience burst into enthusiastic applause.

Later, the student admitted to Juel that in that moment he had felt the same pressure of incompletion as had some of the scribal editors of Mark who provided longer conclusions to the Gospel, a hunger to provide some kind of ending other than fear and silence, some sense of closure, some satisfying resolution. The next time he performed Mark, though, he resisted the temptation to resolve the dangling ending. After saying the last line, he paused for a few dramatic seconds and then silently exited. There was no applause. Instead, "discomfort and uncertainty within the audience were obvious, and as people exited the sanctuary the buzz of conversation was dominated by the experience of non-ending."[32]

"Nobody knows who I am until you get to the cross and the empty tomb." Tick tock.

What characterizes much of our culture (and much of our preaching) is that we have tick, . . . but we are not expecting tock, not hoping for tock. This is especially true, I suspect, in an affluent society that is basically satisfied with the status quo and wishes for an unbroken trajectory from tick, uninterrupted by a tock. As scientist-theologian John Polkinghorne has claimed, much of what counts for hope in the current social context is "in a negative form—as a desire that certain things not occur."[33] I hope the stock market doesn't crash, I hope I don't go into a vegetative state and die in a nursing home, I hope we don't have another 9/11. This is finally a secular hope, a hope that the party will go on forever, which Kierkegaard recognized as the despair that doesn't even know it is despairing, the "sickness unto death." Thy kingdom come, thy will be done?—Oh I hope not.

For persons, what finally breaks up the party, of course, is death. And here is a problem with not preaching eschatologically, with not having a robust eschatological vision that embraces social justice and the restoration of all things in Christ. It is somewhat hollow to be silent on the large eschatological themes, and then suddenly to start speaking eschatologically at the graveside. Here is the opening prayer from the funeral service in the new Evangelical Lutheran Church in America service book. Observe how much this prayer depends upon an embracing eschatological vision:

> O God of grace and glory, we remember before you today our sister/brother, *name*. We thank you for giving her/him to us to know and to love as a companion in our pilgrimage on earth. In your boundless compassion, console us who mourn. Give us faith to see that death has been swallowed up in the victory of our Lord Jesus Christ, so that we may live in confidence and hope until, by your call, we are gathered to our heavenly home in the company of all your saints; through Jesus Christ, our Savior and Lord.[34]

To speak this prayer at a funeral in the presence of people who have not been nourished on a vision of life and faith that is fully eschatological can eviscerate the prayer of its meaning and power. If we have not been preaching the sweeping eschatological vision of the fullness of God that swallows up all forms of death in Christ, this prayer, I fear, can only sound like a "precious little promise."

3. Third, preaching eschatologically today means helping our people know that the eschatological and apocalyptic language of the Bible is not about predicting the future; it is primarily a way of seeing the present in the light of hope. American church historian Brooks Holifield once preached a sermon on the eschatological vision of John in Revelation 7:

> Then one of the elders addressed me, saying, "Who are those, clothed in white robes and whence have they come?" I said to him, "Sir, you know." And he said to me, "These are they who have come out of the great tribulation; they have washed their robes and made

them white in the blood of the Lamb. Therefore are they before the
throne of God, and serve him night and day within his temple; and
he who sits upon the throne will shelter them with his presence.
They shall hunger no more, neither thirst any more, the sun shall not
strike them, nor any scorching heat, For the Lamb in the midst of
the throne will be their shepherd, and he will guide them to springs
of living water, and God will wipe away every tear from their eyes."

(Rev. 7:13–17 RSV)

In the sermon, Holifield made it clear that the basic effect of this passage is not to teach us about the details of heaven but to change the way
we see the present by shining upon it the light of God's future:

> John wasn't predicting. John was *seeing*. The voice told him to write
> down what he saw. John is dealing with images here, with word-
> pictures that are vivid and concrete and inexplicable. John is appeal-
> ing to our imagination. He's giving us images. Picture it, he is say-
> ing to us. This is what I saw. Picture it. Imagine it.
>
> Look again at the text for today. The great multitude, the tribes,
> the people, the angels, the elders, the four living creatures. And look
> even more closely: the people with white robes. Who are they? Well,
> they're people, John tells us, who have come out of great tribulation,
> they've hungered, and thirsted, and suffered the scorching heat of
> the sun. And John sees them—he looks at them—and he writes it
> down, he gives us the image. In May of 2001, fourteen Mexicans,
> illegal immigrants, died from dehydration and hunger after their
> guides abandoned them in the desert, in the scorching heat of the
> sun, near Yuma, Arizona. They passed quickly in and out of our
> lives with two minutes of television images, and they became
> abstract examples of "the illegal immigration problem."
>
> It's hard to imagine their deaths. It's even harder to imagine their
> lives, the hopes that drove them across that border, into that desert,
> the families they left behind, the people they loved and who loved
> them, the ordinariness of their everyday lives. It's hard to see them,
> to look at them, to imagine them.
>
> I don't know if we would change our immigration policies if we
> could learn how to imagine their lives. I don't know. But if we could
> learn to think like John of Patmos thinks—if we could think with
> imagination, if we could hold the images before us, we would see
> things we don't see now and know things we don't know now—and
> perhaps even do things we don't do now.
>
> Blessed are those, Jesus says in Matthew, who hunger and thirst
> for righteousness. Blessed are those, Jesus says in Luke, who hunger.

I see the hungry and the thirsty gathered round the throne, says John of Patmos. These people must occupy a special place in God's reign, the hungry and the thirsty.[35]

As for eschatology enabling people to see the world differently and, thus, to form a deeply Christian ethical response, Charles Campbell, who teaches at Duke Divinity School, reports:

Two years ago, shortly after Labor Day, I was standing on a platform waiting for a subway train in Atlanta. As I was waiting, a homeless man whom I had met hailed me from across the platform and came to stand with me. He reminded me of his name, Michael (like the angel), and we struck up a conversation. Michael told me about his ongoing search for a job and gave thanks for the many ways God was caring for him. When the train arrived, we boarded, sat down together, and continued our conversation.

At one point I asked Michael where he had eaten lunch on Labor Day—a difficult day for homeless people in Atlanta because many services are closed. He told me he had eaten lunch at "910" (short-hand for the Open Door Community, a Christian community that serves food to about 400 people each Labor Day). Michael's eyes widened as he described the large helpings of "real pinto beans" and the generous portions of corn bread—"this thick," he showed me, holding his thumb and forefinger about two inches apart. When he paused, I asked him how many people were at the meal. He stared at me for a moment, and then announced in a loud voice for everyone to hear: "Thousands! There were thousands! They came from the north and the south and the east and the west. There were thousands!"

In the midst of the social and moral death that is homelessness, Michael had discerned the great messianic banquet in pinto beans and corn bread shared among the poor. . . . And as he spoke in that crowded subway car, the powers were put in their place, and we were set free, even if only for a moment, from the bondage of death.[36]

If Jesus is Lord, if Jesus is raised from the dead, then this puts eschatological pressure on the present. All that damages human life is obsolete, passing away, and the preacher can stand up there boldly speaking in the future-present tense. As William Stringfellow urged:

In the face of death, live humanly. In the middle of chaos, celebrate the Word. Amidst babel . . . speak the truth. Confront the noise and verbiage and falsehood of death with the truth and potency and efficacy of the Word of God. Know the Word, teach the Word, nurture the Word, defend the Word, incarnate the Word, do the Word, live the Word. And more than that, in the Word of God expose death and all death's works and wiles, rebuke lies, cast out demons, exorcise, cleanse the possessed, raise those who are dead in mind and conscience.[37]

I was fascinated and moved to read the obituary for Rabbi Hugo Gryn, one of Great Britain's most respected rabbis. When he was a boy, he and his family were imprisoned at Auschwitz. They were Orthodox, and even though it meant even greater danger to them, Hugo's father insisted they observe the Sabbath and the festivals. Hugo remembered until the day he died a time when, to observe the Sabbath, his father took a piece of string and put it in a bit of butter and lit it to make a *shabat* candle. Hugo was furious and protested, "Father, that is all the butter we have!"

His father said, "Without food we can live for weeks. But we cannot live for a minute without hope."

Notes

Chapter 1: A Likely Story

1. Anatole Broyard, *Intoxicated by My Illness* (New York: Fawcett Columbine, 1992), 20.

2. Stanley Kubrick, as quoted in T. A. Nelson, *Kubrick: Inside a Film Artist's Maze* (Bloomington: Indiana University Press, 1982), 250.

3. Fred B. Craddock, *Overhearing the Gospel: Preaching and Teaching the Faith to Persons Who Have Already Heard* (Nashville: Abingdon Press, 1978), 9.

4. Edmund Steimle, Morris J. Niedenthal, and Charles L. Rice, *Preaching the Story* (Philadelphia: Fortress Press, 1980), 12–13.

5. David S. Reynolds, "From Doctrine to Narrative: The Rise of Pulpit Storytelling in America," *American Quarterly* 32/5 (Winter 1980): 479–98.

6. Ibid., 485–86.

7. Ibid., 489.

8. Ralph Waldo Emerson, "Divinity School Address," delivered before the senior class in Divinity College, Cambridge, Sunday evening, July 15, 1838.

9. Quoted in Reynolds, "From Doctrine to Narrative," 480.

10. Ronald E. Sleeth, *God's Word and Our Words: Basic Homiletics* (Atlanta: John Knox Press, 1986), 44.

11. Richard Lischer, "The Limits of Story," *Interpretation* 38/1 (Jan. 1984): 36.

12. James W. Thompson, *Preaching Like Paul: Homiletical Wisdom for Today* (Louisville, KY: Westminster John Knox Press, 2001), 9–14.

13. Susan Wise Bauer, "Stories and Syllogisms: Protestant Hymns, Narrative Theology, and Heresy," in Richard J. Mouw and Mark A. Noll, eds., *Wonderful Words of Life: Hymns in American Protestant History and Theology* (Grand Rapids: Wm. B. Eerdmans, 2004), 232.

14. Charles L. Campbell, *Preaching Jesus: New Directions for Homiletics in Hans Frei's Postliberal Theology* (Grand Rapids: Wm. B. Eerdmans, 1997), 192–93.

15. John S. McClure, *Other-wise Preaching: A Postmodern Ethic for Homiletics* (St. Louis: Chalice Press, 2001), 81.

16. Galen Strawson, "Against Narrativity," *Ratio* (n.s.) 17/4 (Dec. 2004): 428–52.

17. Ibid., 428.

18. Ibid.

19. Ibid., 429.

20. Ibid., 430–31.

21. Ibid., 432–33.

22. Ibid., 433.

23. Ibid., 432.

24. Diana Schaub, "The Greatness and Decline of American Oratory," *Claremont Review of Books* 7/3 (Summer 2007), http://www.claremont.org/publications/crb/id.1393/article_detail.asp.

25. Fleming Rutledge, *The Undoing of Death* (Grand Rapids: Wm. B. Eerdmans, 2005), 14.

26. Ibid., 15.

27. Ibid., 15–16.

28. H. Richard Niebuhr, "The Story of Our Life," excerpted from *The Meaning of Revelation*, in Stanley Hauerwas and L. Gregory Jones, eds., *Why Narrative? Readings in Narrative Theology* (Grand Rapids: Wm. B. Eerdmans, 1989), 42.

29. A version of this story appears in Thomas G. Long, *Testimony: Talking Ourselves into Being Christian* (San Francisco: Jossey-Bass, 2004), 133.

30. B. A. Gerrish, *Grace and Gratitude: The Eucharistic Theology of John Calvin* (Minneapolis: Fortress Press, 1993), 89.

31. Stanley Hauerwas and David Burrell, "From System to Story: An Alternative Pattern for Rationality in Ethics," in Hauerwas and Jones, *Why Narrative?* 190.

32. Michael Welker, "Resurrection and Eternal Life: The Canonic Memory of the Resurrected Christ, His Reality, and His Glory," in John Polkinghorne and Michael Welker, eds., *The End of the World and the Ends of God: Science and Theology on Eschatology* (Harrisburg, PA: Trinity Press Int., 2000), 287.

33. *Didascalia* 2.58.6, as cited in Gordon Lathrop, *Holy Things: A Liturgical Theology* (Minneapolis: Fortress Press, 1993), 120.

34. Paul Ricoeur, *Time and Narrative* (Chicago: University of Chicago Press, 1984), 1:75.

35. Rebecca Chopp, "Theology and the Poetics of Testimony," *Criterion* 37/1 (Winter 1998): 2.

36. Elizabeth A. Johnson, *Friends of Gods and Prophets: A Feminist Theological Reading of the Communion of Saints* (New York: Continuum, 2003), 248–49.

37. Meir Sternberg, *The Poetics of Biblical Narrative* (Bloomington: Indiana University Press, 1985), 47.

38. Robert Alter, *The Art of Biblical Narrative* (New York: Basic Books, 1981), 33.

39. Ibid.

40. Oliver Sacks, *The Man Who Mistook His Wife for a Hat and Other Clinical Tales* (New York: Touchstone, 1998), 37–38.

41. Ibid., 39.

Chapter 2: No News Is Bad News

1. John Barton, *The Nature of Biblical Criticism* (Louisville, KY: Westminster John Knox Press, 2007), 190.

2. John M. Todd, *Luther: A Life* (New York: Crossroad, 1982), 41–42.

3. Ibid., 42.

4. Ibid.

5. As cited in Erik H. Erikson, *Young Man Luther: A Study in Psychoanalysis and History* (New York: W. W. Norton, 1993, first published in 1953), 59.

6. Luther, as quoted in Todd, 42–43.

7. Ibid., 140.

8. Ibid., 145

9. Peter Berger, *The Heretical Imperative: Contemporary Possibilities of Religious Affirmation* (Garden City, NY: Anchor Press, 1979), 54–55.

10. Terry Eagleton, "Lunging, Flailing, Mispunching," *London Review of Books* 28/20 (Oct. 19, 2006): 32.

11. Charles Taylor, *A Secular Age* (Cambridge, MA: Belknap Press, 2007), 22.

12. Ibid., 3

13. Taylor, *A Secular Age*, 28.

14. Karl Barth, *The Word of God and the Word of Man*, trans. Douglas Horton (New York: Harper & Row, 1957), 125–26, emphasis in the original.

15. George W. Stroup, *Before God* (Grand Rapids: Wm. B. Eerdmans, 2004), 181.

16. Garrett Keizer, *A Dresser of Sycamore Trees: The Finding of a Ministry* (New York: Viking, 1991), 73.

17. David F. Ford, *Christian Wisdom: Desiring God and Learning in Love* (Cambridge: Cambridge University Press, 2007), 5, emphasis in the original.

18. Annie Dillard, *Teaching a Stone to Talk: Expeditions and Encounters* (New York: Harper, 1982), 52.

19. William Harmless, *Augustine and the Catechumenate* (Collegeville, MN: Liturgical Press, 1995), see esp. chap. 5.

20. Ibid., 161.

21. Ibid., 162.

22. Secundicus, *Ad sanctum Augustinum epistula 3*, as quoted in William Harmless, *Augustine and the Catechumenate* (Collegeville, MN: Liturgical Press, 1995), 164.

23. Peter Brown, *Augustine of Hippo: A Biography* (Berkeley: University of California Press, 1967), 268.

24. Possidius, *Vita 31*, and cited in Harmless, *Augustine and the Catechumenate,* 166.

25. Harmless, *Augustine and the Catechumenate,* 168.

26. Ibid., 169.

27. Ibid.

28. Augustine, *Sermo 96.4*, as quoted in Harmless, *Augustine and the Catechumenate,* 169.

29. Augustine, *De doctrina christiana 4.6.10*, trans. R. P. H. Green and published as *On Christian Teaching* (New York: Oxford, 1997), 107.

30. Augustine, *Sermo 95.1*, as quoted in Harmless, *Augustine and the Catechumenate,* 160–61.

31. Augustine, *Sermo 17.2*, as quoted in Harmless, *Augustine and the Catechumenate,* 188.

32. George Steiner, *Real Presences* (Chicago: University of Chicago Press, 1989), 3–4.

33. Ibid.

34. George Steiner, "Books: The Good Book," *New Yorker*, Jan. 11, 1988, 94.

35. Ibid., 97

36. Michael Fishbane, *Text and Texture* (New York: Schocken Books, 1979).

37. Robert Alter, *The Art of Biblical Narrative* (New York: Basic Books, 1981), 16.

38. Daniel Patte, *Preaching Paul*, Fortress Resources for Preaching (Philadelphia: Fortress Press, 1984), 61, 77.

39. Garrett Green, *Imagining God: Theology and the Religious Imagination* (San Francisco: Harper & Row, 1989), 107.

40. The following discussion is drawn from Paul Ricoeur, *Time and Narrative* (Chicago: University of Chicago Press, 1984), 1:5–87.

41. Ibid., 74–75.

42. I say that preaching begins at the level of *mimesis1* "in a sense," and only in a sense, because, despite the fragmentation of contemporary experience, congregations do not suffer from total amnesia. They have heard the gospel before, and they remember from week to week that they are part of an ongoing gospel narrative, however imperiled that may be. Preaching both starts anew each time, and does not.

43. Ricoeur, *Time and Narrative*, 80.

44. Ibid., 77.

45. Robert Wuthnow, "Stories to Live By," *Theology Today* 49/3 (Oct. 1992): 308.

46. See the important discussion of this text, from which many of the insights here are drawn, in Robert Tannehill, *The Sword of His Mouth* (Missoula, MT: Scholar's Press, 1975), 118–22.

Chapter 3: Nasty Suspicions, Conspiracy Theories, and the Return of Gnosticism

1. Christopher Hitchens, *God Is Not Great: How Religion Poisons Everything* (New York: Twelve Books, 2007), 115.

2. Edward Farley, *Ecclesial Man: A Social Phenomenology of Faith and Reality* (Philadelphia: Fortress, 1975), 6.

3. Farley argues for a different chronology, namely that, at least tacitly, the church developed a loss of confidence in the reality of its faith language before the theological academy picked up the theme. Perhaps in a subtle way this is true. As an explicitly pastoral and homiletical problem, however, lay people are now posing challenges to the traditional formulations of faith using books, discoveries, theories, and categories first generated in the academy.

4. Bart D. Ehrman, *Lost Christianities: The Battles for Scripture and the Faiths We Never Knew* (New York: Oxford, 203), 3.

5. Discovery Channel press release, February 25, 2007, archived at http://dsc.discovery.com/news/2007/02/25/tomb_arc.html?category'archaeology.

6. Robert Funk, "Opening Remarks at the First Meeting of the Jesus Seminar, March 21–24, 1985," *Forum* 1/1 (1985): 8.

7. Ibid.

8. Laurie Goodstein, "Document Is Genuine, but Is Its Story True?" *New York Times*, April 7, 2006, A20.

9. Marcus Borg, *The Heart of Christianity: Rediscovering a Life of Faith* (San Francisco: HarperSanFrancisco, 2003), xi.

10. Ibid., 2.

11. John Shelby Spong, *Christianity for the Non-Religious* (New York: Harper One, 2007), xi–xii.

12. Elaine Pagels, *Beyond Belief: The Secret Gospel of Thomas* (New York: Vintage, 2004).

13. I am not the only observer connecting the current quest for spirituality to the gnostic movement in early Christianity. See, for example, Harold Bloom, *The American Religion: The Emergence of the Post-Christian Nation* (New York: Simon & Schuster, 1992); Jeremy Lott, "American Gnostic: Harold Bloom's 'Post-Christian Nation' Ten Years On," *Books and Culture,* 8/6 (Nov.-Dec. 2002): 36; Owen C. Thomas, "Spiritual but Not Religious: The Influence of the Current Romantic Movement," *Anglican Theological Review* 88/3 (Summer 2006): 397–415; Luke Timothy Johnson, "A New Gnosticism: An Old Threat to the Church," *Commonweal* (Nov. 5, 2004): 28–31; N. T. Wright, *Judas and the Gospel of Jesus: Have We Missed the Truth about Christianity?* (Grand Rapids: Baker Books, 2006), and esp. Philip J. Lee, *Against the Protestant Gnostics* (New York: Oxford University Press, 1987).

14. Raymond E. Brown, "The Christians Who Lost Out," a review of Elaine Pagels, *The Gnostic Gospels, New York Times*, Jan. 20, 1980, 3.

15. Bloom's wild and iconoclastic *The American Religion* describes "the American Religion" as "irretrievably Gnostic." Bloom's definition of gnosticism, though more negative and extreme than I would like, does see gnosticism in dynamic rather than strictly doctrinal terms: "It is a knowing, by and of an uncreated self, or self-within-the-self, and the knowledge leads to freedom, a dangerous and doom-eager freedom: from nature, time, history, community, other selves" (49).

16. Elaine Pagels, *The Gnostic Gospels* (New York: Random House, 1979), 150.

17. Ioan P. Culianu, "The Gnostic Revenge: Gnosticism and Romantic Literature," in *Religionstheorie und Politische Theologie*, vol. 2, *Gnosis und Politik* (Munich: Wilhelm Funk/Ferdinand Schöningh, 1984), 290.

18. See, for example, Karen L. King, *What Is Gnosticism?* (Cambridge, MA: Belknap Press, 2003) and Michael Allen Williams, *Rethinking "Gnosticism": An Argument for Dismantling a Dubious Category* (Princeton, NJ: Princeton University Press, 1996).

19. Bryan K. Sholl, review of Cyril O'Regan, *Gnostic Return in Modernity and Gnostic Apocalypse: Jacob Boehme's Haunted Narrative*, in *Pro Ecclesia* 13/2 (Sept. 2004): 245.

20. Van Austin Harvey, *The Historian and the Believer: The Morality of Historical Knowledge and Christian Belief* (New York: Macmillan, 1969), 103.

21. Lee, *Against the Protestant Gnostics,* 5.

22. Pagels, *The Gnostic Gospels,* 149.

23. Pagels, *The Gnostic Gospels,* 118.

24. Bart D. Ehrman, *Lost Christianities,* 4.

25. Kathleen McVey, "Gnosticism, Feminism, and Elaine Pagels," *Theology Today* 37/4 (Jan. 1981): 499.

26. Tom Hall, personal correspondence with Karen L. King, as cited in King, *What Is Gnosticism?* 8.

27. James M. Robinson is helpful when he points out that, in regard to the earliest church, "*heresy* and *orthodoxy* are anachronistic." Rather, what came to be called "heresy" and "orthodoxy" were the result of developing attempts to make sense of "a common body of beliefs variously understood." What is perhaps underemphasized here, however, is the pastoral element in this process. Views did not endure and become "orthodox" because they "won" rather than "lost," but because they brought richer life and deeper meaning to Christian communities. See James M. Robinson and Helmut Koester, *Trajectories through Early Christianity* (Philadelphia: Fortress Press, 1971), 62, 69.

28. Arthur Darby Nock, "Gnosticism," *Harvard Theological Review* 57/4 (Oct. 1964): 273.

29. Brown, "The Christians Who Lost Out," 33.

30. Lee, *Against the Protestant Gnostics,* 5

31. Luke Timothy Johnson, "A New Gnosticism," 31.

32. N. T. Wright, *Judas and the Gospel of Jesus,* 94–95.

33. My list is somewhat different from, but is nonetheless suggested by, a similar list in Lee, *Against the Protestant Gnostics*, 16–44.

34. Birger A. Pearson, *Ancient Gnosticism: Traditions and Literature* (Minneapolis: Fortress Press, 2007), 12.

35. Ross Douthat, "Lord Have Mercy," *Claremont Review of Books* 7/3 (Summer, 2007), http://www.claremont.org/publications/crb/id.1396/article_detail.asp.

36. Bart D. Ehrman in Rodolphe Kasser et al., eds., *The Gospel of Judas* (Washington: National Geographic, 2006), 110.

37. John Shelby Spong, "The Easter Moment: Drawing Conclusions," www.beliefnet.com/story/76/story_7622_2.html.

38. Bloom, *The American Religion*, 49.

39. As quoted in Pagels, *The Gnostic Gospels*, ix–xx.

40. Jim Harrison, *True North* (New York: Grove Press, 2004), 299.

41. Ibid., 360.

42. See, for example, Malcolm L. Peel, "Gnostic Eschatology and the New Testament," *Novum Testamentum* 12/2 (April 1970): 141–65.

43. *Gospel of Thomas,* logion 51, from Stephen Patterson and Marvin Meyer, *The Scholars' Translation of the Gospel of Thomas,* http://users.misericordia.edu//davies/thomas/Trans.htm, emphasis mine.

44. Lee, *Against the Protestant Gnostics*, 4.

45. Nock, "Gnosticism," 277.

Chapter 4: Meeting Marcus Borg Again for the First Time

1. Harvey, *The Historian and the Believer* (New York: Macmillan, 1969), 103.

2. Borg, *The Heart of Christianity* (San Francisco: HarperSanFrancisco, 2003), 39.

3. Martin Buber, *The Eclipse of God* (New York: Harper & Bros., 1952), 175.

4. Bloom, *The American Religion* (New York: Simon & Schuster, 1992), 22.

5. Ibid.

6. Ibid., 15.

7. "He Lives!" Words and Music by Alfred H. Ackley, copyright 1933, Homer A. Rodeheaver, renewal 1961, by The Rodeheaver Co. (Word Music, Inc.) and currently held by Warner Chappell Music Inc., Los Angeles, CA.

8. Jeremy Lott, "American Gnostic: Harold Bloom's 'Post-Christian Nation' Ten Years On," *Books and Culture* 8/6 (Nov.–Dec. 2002): 36.

9. John Shelby Spong, *Jesus for the Non-Religious* (New York; HarperCollins, 2007), 293.

10. Cyril O'Regan, *Gnostic Return in Modernity* (Albany: State University of New York Press, 2001), 182–84.

11. O'Regan is specifically working on what he calls the narrative grammar of Valentinian gnosticism, a variety that developed in the Hellenistic period. His list of ideological conditions names circumstances that must be in place "if Valentinian narrative grammar is to be exercised beyond the Hellenistic field" (182). The use of this list to understand neo-gnostic trends in contemporary Christianity goes beyond O'Regan's scope and represents my own reapplication of his categories. I have paraphrased most of O'Regan's list, given them my own labels, and added one entry, #3.

12. Borg, *The Heart of Christianity*, xi.

13. Marcus Borg, *Meeting Jesus Again for the First Time: The Historical Jesus and the Heart of Contemporary Faith* (San Francisco: HarperSanFrancisco, 1995).

14. Borg, *The Heart of Christianity*, xii.

15. Ibid., 13–14.

16. Marcus Borg, "Seeing Jesus: Sources, Lenses, and Method," in Marcus J. Borg and N. T. Wright, *The Meaning of Jesus: Two Visions* (San Francisco: HarperSanFrancisco, 2000), 14.

17. Ibid.

18. Ibid.

19. Borg, *Meeting Jesus Again for the First Time*, 29.

20. Ibid.

21. Borg, *The Heart of Christianity,* 171–72.

22. Ibid., 173.

23. James D. G. Dunn, *A New Perspective on Jesus: What the Quest for the Historical Jesus Missed* (Grand Rapids: Baker Academic, 2005), 29.

24. Ibid., 5.

25. Borg, *The Heart of Christianity*, 67.

26. Ibid., 18.

27. See esp. Marcus J. Borg, *The God We Never Knew: Beyond Dogmatic Religion to a More Authentic Contemporary Faith* (San Francisco: HarperSanFrancisco, 1997), chap. 3.

28. Marcus Borg, *Jesus: Uncovering the Life, Teaching, and Relevance of a Religious Revolutionary* (San Francisco: HarperSanFrancisco, 2006), 295.

29. Ibid.

30. Borg, *The God We Never Knew*, 61–79.

31. O'Regan, *Gnostic Return in Modernity*, 2.

32. Borg, *Meeting Jesus Again for the First Time*, 6.

33. Borg, *The Heart of Christianity*, 171–72.

34. Ibid., 181–84.

35. Borg, *Meeting Jesus Again for the First Time*, 9.

36. Borg, *The Heart of Christianity*, 43.

37. Ibid., 172–75.

38. Ibid., 183.

39. Ibid., 184.

40. Birger A. Pearson, *Ancient Gnosticism: Traditions and Literature* (Minneapolis: Fortress Press, 2007), 12.

41. John Shelby Spong, *The Sins of Scripture: Exposing the Bible's Texts of Hate to Reveal the God of Love* (New York: HarperOne, 2005), 179.

42. Lee, *Against the Protestant Gnostics*, 21.

43. Borg, *Meeting Jesus Again for the First Time*, 9.

44. Ibid., 87.

45. Ibid., 88.

46. I have myself told a version of this sentimental story in a sermon long ago, for which I now repent in dust and ashes.

47. Borg, *The Heart of Christianity*, 114.

48. Ibid., 117.

49. Ibid., 120, emphasis in the original.

50. Pearson, *Ancient Gnosticism*, 13.

51. "Gather Us In," words by Monty Haugen, copyright 1982 by GIA Publications, Inc.

52. Borg, *Meeting Jesus Again for the First Time*, 87.

53. Neale Donald Walsch, *Conversations with God: An Uncommon Dialogue, Boook 2* (Charlottesville, VA: Hampton Roads Publishers, 1997), 249.

54. Recreation Foundation, "Conversations with God," Recreation Foundation, http://www.cwg.org/main.php?p'Neale&sub'Story.

55. Borg, *The Heart of Christianity*, 65–66, emphasis in the original. Borg has borrowed these two views of God from Karen Armstrong's *A History of God*. In his *The God We Never Knew*, Borg again presents two contrasting images of God, but

names different images, in this case the "Monarchical Model" versus "God as Spirit" (61–79). The discussions of the contrasting models in the two books, however, is quite similar.

56. Ibid., 69.

57. Eagleton, "Lunging, Flailing, Mispunching," 32.

58. Ibid., 196–97.

59. See "A Test Case: Divine Action," in Christopher Southgate et al., *God, Humanity, and the Cosmos: A Textbook in Science and Religion* (Harrisburg, PA: Trinity Press Int., 1999), 245–83.

60. Borg, *The Heart of Christianity*, 67.

61. Ibid., 219.

62. Ibid.

63. Ibid., 218–19.

64. Ibid., 218.

65. Richard B. Hays, "The Corrected Jesus," *First Things* 43 (May 1994): 43.

66. Borg, *Meeting Jesus Again for the First Time*, 29.

67. Borg, *Jesus*, 76.

68. Hays, "The Corrected Jesus," 47.

69. Borg, *Meeting Jesus Again for the First Time*, 22.

70. Ibid., 25–61.

71. Ulrich Luz, *Matthew 8–20: A Commentary* (Minneapolis: Fortress Press, 2001), 282.

72. Martin Kähler, *The So-Called Historical Jesus and the Historic Biblical Christ* (Philadelphia: Fortress Press, 1964).

73. George Tyrell, *Christianity at the Crossroads* (London: George Allen, 1909), 44.

74. Paul Ricoeur, "From Proclamation to Narrative," *Journal of Religion* 64/4 (Oct. 1984): 502.

75. Ehrman, *Lost Christianities*, 256–57.

76. Luke Timothy Johnson, "A New Gnosticism: An Old Threat to the Church," *Commonweal* (Nov. 5, 2004): 30.

77. Christopher Morse, *Not Every Spirit: A Dogmatics of Christian Disbelief* (Valley Forge, PA: Trinity Press Int., 1994), 3.

Chapter 5: Preaching in the Future-Prefect Tense

1. Anatole Broyard, *Intoxicated by My Illness* (New York: Fawcett Columbine, 1992), 66.

2. James H. Moorhead, *World without End: Mainstream Protestant Visions of the Last Things, 1880–1925* (Bloomington: Indiana University Press, 1999), 11.

3. *United Presbyterian A.D.* (Oct. 1981), 16 as quoted in J. Christiaan Beker, *Paul's Apocalyptic Gospel: The Coming Triumph of God* (Philadelphia: Fortress Press, 1982), 12–13.

4. *United Presbyterian A.D.* (Dec. 1981), 8, as quoted in Beker, 13.

5. Moorhead, *World without End*, xiii.

6. Ibid., xii.

7. Ibid., xiv.

8. Ibid.

9. John Barton, *Reading the Old Testament: Method in Biblical Study*, 2nd ed. (Louisville, KY: Westminster John Knox Press, 1994), 17.

10. James Turner, *Without God, without Creed* (Baltimore: Johns Hopkins University Press, 1985), 155.

11. Edmund Gosse, *Father and Son: A Study of Two Temperaments* (New York: W. W. Norton, 1963, original ed. 1907), 231–32, as quoted in Moorhead, *World without End*, xi.

12. Ernst Troeltsch, as quoted in F. L. Polak, *The Image of the Future* (New York: Oceana Publications, 1961), 243.

13. See John B. Cobb Jr., *Christ in a Pluralistic Age* (Philadelphia: Westminster Press, 1975), chap. 1.

14. Turner, *Without God, without Creed*, 237.

15. Woody Allen, "God: A Play," in *Without Feathers* (New York: Random House, 1975), 173–75.

16. Turner, *Without God, without Creed*, xiii.

17. "Gather Us In," words by Marty Haugen, copyright 1982 by GIA Publications, Inc.

18. Marcus Borg, *The Heart of Christianity: Rediscovering a Life of Faith* (San Francisco: Harper Collins, 2003), 173.

19. Ibid., 178, emphasis mine.

20. Ibid., 172, emphasis mine.

21. Beker, *Paul's Apocalyptic Gospel*, 118.

22. Cormac McCarthy, *No Country for Old Men* (New York: Vintage, 2006), 218.

23. Ibid., 296.

24. Ibid., 308.

25. Ibid., 309.

26. *The Shawshank Redemption: The Shooting Script*, screenplay and notes by Frank Darabont, intro. by Stephen King (New York: Newmarket Press, 1996), 61–62.

27. Gayraud S. Wilmore, *Last Things First* (Philadelphia: Westminster Press, 1982), 11, emphasis in the original.

28. Karl Barth, *The Epistle to the Romans* (London: Oxford, 1933), 313–14.

29. Ibid., 314.

30. Georges Bernanos, *The Diary of a Country Priest* (New York: Carroll & Graf, 1983), 53.

31. Frank Kermode, *The Sense of an Ending: Studies in the Theory of Fiction* (London: Oxford University Press, 1967), 45–47.

32. Donald H. Juel, *The Gospel of Mark* (Nashville: Abingdon Press, 1999), 172.

33. John Polkinghorne, "Eschatology: Some Questions and Some Insights from Science," in John Polkinghorne and Michael Welker, eds., *The End of the World and the Ends of God: Science and Theology on Eschatology* (Harrisburg, PA: Trinity Press Int., 2000), 41.

34. *Evangelical Lutheran Worship, Pew Edition* (Minneapolis: Augsburg Fortress, 2006), 281. The funeral prayer originally appeared in *Life Passages: Renewing Worship*, volume 4, copyright by the Evangelical Lutheran Church in America and administered by Augsburg Fortress Publishers. Used by permission of Augsburg Fortress Publishers.

35. Brooks Holifield, a sermon preached at Cannon Chapel, Emory University.

36. Charles Campbell, "Principalities, Powers, and Preaching: Learning from William Stringfellow," *Interpretation* 51/4 (Oct. 1997), 395–96.

37. William Stringfellow, *An Ethic for Christians and Other Aliens in a Strange Land* (Waco, TX: Word Books, 1973), 142–43.

Index

Abilene Christian University, 8
Academy of Homiletics, 7–8
Acts of the Apostles, 61, 109
Adam and Eve, 94
African Americans, 19–20, 34–35,
    110, 126
afterlife. *See* eschatology
"Against Narrativity" (Strawson), 10
agnosticism, 117
Akhmatova, Anna, 22
Allen, Woody, 118
All Saints, 22
Alter, Robert, 23–24
American Religion, The (Bloom), 79–80
Anthropology, 116
"antinarrative sermons," 14–15
apocalypticism, 114–15. *See also*
    eschatology
Apostles' Creed, 81, 125
Arian controversy, 59
Aristotle, 45–46
Armstrong, Karen, 62, 63–64, 83,
    140n55
As One without Authority (Craddock), 3
atheism, 79, 117–18
Atlantic Monthly, 73
Augustine, 5–6, 18, 39–41, 45–46
Augustine and the Catechumenate
    (Harmless), 39

baptism, 11
Baptist Church, 19–20, 113
Barth, Karl, 35, 124
Barton, John, 27, 115
Bauer, Susan Wise, 8–9
Beecher, Henry Ward, 6
Beecher, Lyman, 112

Beker, J. Christian, 119
Berger, Peter, 30
Bernano, Georges, 126
Beyond Belief (Pagels), 64
Bible
    ambiguity and complexity of
        narratives of, 23
    apocalypticism and, 114–15
    Borg on, 85–86, 90
    Calvin on, 44
    exegesis and, 42–45, 50–53
    German higher criticism of, 116
    intelligent understanding of, by lay
        Christians, 56–58, 61–63
    literal and factual accuracy of, 115,
        116, 123
    literary criticism of the Bible,
        41–42
    purpose of, 23
    Ricoeur on, 24
    spiritual interpretation of, 82–83
    tension in, 23
    wisdom and, 37–38
    See also specific books of the Bible
blasphemy, 97
Bloom, Harold, 75, 79–80, 137n15
body
    antipathy toward, 72–74, 95–103
    Word became flesh, 32, 73, 96
    See also incarnation
Borg, Marcus J.
    on afterlife, 86, 89–90, 119
    on antipathy toward incarnation and
        embodiment, 98–103
    childhood religious beliefs of, 89,
        92–94, 98
    on Christianity seen as a whole, 86

Borg, Marcus J. (*continued*)
  and conditions for return of gnostic
    impulse, 85–87
  on eschatology, 86, 90
  on evil, 86
  gnostic impulse and, 89–106
  on God, 87, 88, 90, 94–95, 98–100,
    140n55
  The Heart of Christianity by, 62, 79
  on historical Jesus, 85–88, 90, 92–94,
    102–6
  on history and culture, 100–101
  liberalism and, 88, 89
  Meeting Jesus Again for the First Time
    by, 85
  orthodoxy and, 88–89
  on pantheism, 98–101
  reasons for focus on, 83–85
  on religious pluralism, 101
  on religious traditions, 101–2
  and renewed gnostic impulse gener-
    ally, 63–64, 78, 81
  on salvation and this world, 119
  on salvation by gnosis (knowledge),
    90–94
  on scriptures, 85–86, 90
  on spiritual inner self or divine spark
    within, 94–95
  on spirituality, 101
  on suffering, 86
  on traditional versus emerging Chris-
    tianity, 62, 86–88
  See also gnosticism
Brooks, David, 73
Brooks, Phillips, 6
Brown, Dan, 58, 60
Brown, Peter, 39
Brown, Raymond, 65, 71
Brown v. the Board of Education, 19
Broyard, Anatole, 1, 111
Buber, Martin, 79, 81
Buechner, Frederick, 5, 38, 41
Burrell, David, 21

California, 119–20
Calvin, John, 20, 44
Campbell, Charles L., 9, 131

Carlin, George, 111
Carolinas, 29–30
Casey, Jack, 49
Catholic Church, 22, 39, 60, 118–19
Catholic Theological Union, 60
cerebral palsy, 29–30
children with disabilities, 29–30
Chopp, Rebecca, 22
Christ. *See* Jesus Christ
Christianity
  Borg on Christianity seen as a
    whole, 86
  Borg on traditional versus emerging
    Christianity, 62, 86–88
  superiority of, to other religions,
    115–16
  See also eschatology; faith; gnosticism;
    preaching; and *specific churches*
Christian Wisdom (Ford), 38
Cicero, 5
civil rights movement, 19–20, 110
Commager, Henry Steele, 7
Communion. *See* Eucharist
Comparative study of religions, 116
Confessions, The (Augustine), 45
configuration, 47, 48–49
Congregational Church, 113
conservatism, 8–9, 12. *See also*
  evangelicals; and *specific theologians*
conspiracy theories, 58–61
"Conversations with God" (Walsch), 97
Corinthians, First Epistle to, 36, 70, 77
Corinthians, Second Epistle to, 49, 96
Cornell University, 116
Council of Nicaea, 59, 70
Craddock, Fred B., 3, 5, 9, 14
crucifixion, 15–17, 71, 93
Culianu, Ioan, 66

Darwin, Charles, 62, 116, 118
Da Vinci Code, The (Brown), 58, 60
Davis, H. Grady, 3
Dawkins, Richard, 31–32, 98
"The Deacon's Masterpiece, or the
  Wonderful One-Hoss Shay"
  (Holmes), 116
De doctrina christiana (Augustine), 5

Derrida, Jacques, 47
desegregation, 19–20
Design for Preaching (Davis), 3
Diachronics, 11–12, 14
Diary of a Country Priest (Bernano), 126
Didascalia, 21
Dillard, Annie, 38
disabilities, 29–30
Disciple Bible Study, 63
Discovery Channel, 58–59, 60
Douglass, Frederick, 34–35
Douthat, Ross, 73
Dresser of Sycamore Trees, A (Keizer), 36–37
Dunn, James D. G., 86, 106

Eagleton, Terry, 31–32, 98
Easter, 36–37, 70, 71, 74
Ecclesiastes, book of, xiv
Ehrman, Bart D., 62, 63–64, 69, 74, 107
Ellington, Duke, 123
embodiment. *See* body; incarnation
Emerson, 6–7
Enger, Leif, 120
Enlightenment, 32
Ephesians, Epistle to, 80–81
Episcopal Church, 62, 113
Episodics, 12, 14
Erhman, Bart, 57
Erikson, Erik, 28–29, 31
eschatology
    apocalypticism and, 114–15
    Borg on, 86, 90
    characteristics of eschatological preaching, 125–32
    evangelicals and, 119–20
    gnostic focus on present spiritual reality versus, 76–78, 82, 103–6
    hope and, 110, 124, 128–29, 129–32
    Jesus on afterlife, 86, 89–90, 103, 119
    John the Baptist and, 104
    loss of, in preaching, 112–17
    in novels and movies, 120–23
    Paul and, 119
    postmillennialism and, 113–16

progress as replacement for, 117–18
promise of God's *shalom* and, 125–26
providence of God and, 126–29
return of the repressed and, 117–25
systematic theology and, 120
traditional views of, 82
types of, 123
ethical Narrativity thesis, 10–11
Eucharist, 25, 28
Evangelical Lutheran Church in America, 129
evangelicals, 8–9, 12, 79, 119–20
Eve and Adam, 94
evil, 17, 72–73, 82, 86, 99–100, 109, 120–22
evolution theory, 62
exegesis, 42–45, 50–53
Exodus, book of, 36, 50–51

faith, 22–25, 32–34, 36, 38, 80–82, 108–9
the fall, 94
Farley, Edward, 55, 58, 136n3
feminism, 22, 105
Festus, King, 61
Feuerbach, 55
Fishbane, Rabbi Michael, 42–43
Forbes, James, 5
Ford, David F., 38
Fosdick, Harry Emerson, 39
Fox, Matthew, 62
Frei, Hans, 9
Freud, Sigmund, 116
fundamentalism, 79, 101
funeral service, 129
Funk, Robert, 59

Galatians, Epistle to, 17
Gardner, Herb, 43
Genesis, book of, 11, 32
Georgia, 19–21, 125–26, 131
gnosis (knowledge), 64, 72, 77, 90–94.
    See also gnosticism
gnostic Gospels, 56, 60, 66
Gnostic Gospels, The (Pagels), 68–69, 75

gnosticism
    American Christians and, 79–83
    antipathy toward incarnation and
        embodiment and, 72–74, 95–103
    Borg's influence on renewed gnostic
        impulse, 62–64, 78, 79, 81,
        83–106
    Brown on, 65
    Buber on, 79
    conditions for return of gnostic
        impulse, 82–83, 85–87
    as controversial term, 66–67
    definitions of, 65, 137n15
    early Christian gnosticism, 64–65,
        68–72, 77–78, 99–100, 109
    God of, 73, 76–78, 81, 95, 99–100
    and love of God and neighbor, 107–8
    Pagels on suppressed current of, 65
    Paul on, 68, 77
    preaching to neo-gnostics, 106–10
    present spiritual reality and, 76–78,
        103–6
    return of gnostic impulse, 64–68
    salvation by gnosis (knowledge), 64,
        72, 77, 90–94
    and spiritual inner self or divine spark
        within, 74–76, 79–81, 94–95
    themes of contemporary gnosticism,
        72–78
    Valentinian gnosticism, 139n11
    See also Borg, Marcus J.
Gnostic Return in Modernity (O'Regan),
        81–83
God
    of Apostles' Creed, 81
    biblical God, 100
    Borg on, 87, 88, 90, 94–95, 98–100,
        140n55
    contrasting models of, 140n55
    creation by, 96, 100
    Dawkins on, 98
    death of, 118
    existence of, 73
    gnostic view of, 73, 76–78, 81, 95,
        99–100
    intervention by, 99–100
    inward quest for, 74–76, 94–95, 107

    longing for, 38
    love of human beings for, 107
    as mysterium tremendum, 27–32, 79
    pantheism and, 98–101
    Paul on, 99
    presence of, 36–37, 44
    providence of, 126–29
    relationship between human beings
        and, 83, 94–95
    shalom of, 125
    Steiner on, 41
God Delusion, The (Dawkins),
        31–32, 98
good versus evil, 72
Gospels. See specific Gospel, such as Luke,
        Gospel of
Gosse, Edmund, 116–17
Graham, Billy, 79
Green, Garrett, 44
Grier, William Moffatt, xi–x
Gryn, Rabbi Hugo, 132

haggadah, 18
halakah, 18
Harding, Warren, 2
Harmless, William, 39–40
Harnack, Adolf von, 105
Harrison, Jim, 75–76
Harvey, Van, 67, 79
Hauerwas, Stanley, 20–21
Hays, Richard, 102
healing, 29–30
Heart of Christianity, The (Borg), 62, 79
Hebrews, Epistle to, 11
heresy, 67, 138n27
Hijuelos, Oscar, 120
Hippolytus, 68
Hitchens, Christopher, 55
Holifield, Brooks, 129–31
Holmes, Oliver Wendell, 116
Holocaust, 99–100, 127, 132
homelessness, 131
Homiletical Plot, The (Lowry), 3
homiletics, 43
homosexuality, 87
hope, 110, 124, 128–29, 129–32.
        See also eschatology

Ignatius, 68
immanent, 30–31
immortality of the soul, 73–74
incarnation
   antipathy to, 72–74, 93–103
   of Jesus Christ, 92, 96–97, 102
   Word became flesh, 32, 73, 96
   See also body
Irenaeus, 68, 71, 109
Islam, 116

Jesus Christ
   afterlife and, 86, 89–90, 103, 119
   in art, 117
   Borg on, 85–88, 90, 92–94, 102–6
   divinity of, 59, 89, 92–93
   feminist instincts of, 105
   gnostic view of, 64–65, 68, 76
   historical Jesus, 56, 58–59, 85–88,
     90, 92–94, 102–6
   incarnation of, 92, 96–97, 102
   Judaism of, 103–6
   miracles of, 116
   passion story of, 15–17, 71, 93
   Paul on, 96
   personal relationship with, 80
   as pioneer and perfecter of faith, 11
   resurrection of, 37–38, 70, 71, 73–74,
     108–10, 125
   Ricoeur on, 106
   as sage and prophet, 94, 96, 105
   as savior, 92–94
   sayings of, 57
   second coming of, 112–13,
     114, 121
   on wise scribe, xiv
   See also specific gospels
Jesus Seminar, 59, 102, 104
John, First Epistle of, 96
John, Gospel of, 32, 57, 68, 96
John Paul II, Pope, 22
Johnson, Elizabeth, 22
Johnson, Luke, 71, 109
John the Baptist, 104
Judaism, 42–43, 103–6, 123–24, 132
Judas, Gospel of, 60
Juel, Don, 128

justice, 34–35, 37–38, 63, 107–8,
   125, 129
Justin Martyr, 68

Kähler, Martin, 105
Keizer, Garrett, 36–37
Kermode, Frank, 127
Kerygma, 63
Kierkegaard, Søren, 3, 9, 28, 129
King, Martin Luther, 110
knowledge. *See* gnosis (knowledge);
   gnosticism
Kubrick, Stanley, 1

Lee, Philip J., 71, 77, 92
Left Behind series of books, 113
Lessing, 55
Levinas, 10
Levi-Strauss, Claude, 47
liberalism, 9–10, 13, 87–88, 89. *See also*
   specific theologians
Lischer, Richard, 8
Lott, Jeremy, 80
love, 107–8
Lowry, Eugene, 3
Luke, Gospel of, 51–53, 57, 74, 75, 130
Luther, Hans, 27, 28
Luther, Martin, 27–29, 31, 34, 35
Lutheran Church, 89, 93
Luz, Ulrich, 105

Malraux, Andre, 117
Man Who Mistook His Wife for a Hat,
   The (Sacks), 24–25
Mark, Gospel of, 15, 57, 127–28
Mary, Gospel of, 56, 70
Mary Magdalene, 58–59
Mass, 24–25, 27–28
Matthew, Gospel of, xiv, 18, 57, 130
McAdoo, William, 2
McCarthy, Cormac, 120
McClure, John, 10
McVey, Kathleen, 69
Meaning of Life, The, 99
Meeting Jesus Again for the First Time
   (Borg), 85
megachurches, 14–15, 119–20

Methodist Church, 6, 113
Metz, Johann Baptist, 9
mimesis, 45–50, 53, 136n42
mimetic exegesis, 50–53
miracles, 116
Monoimus, 75
Moody, Dwight L., 6
Moorhead, James, 113–15
Mormons, 79–80
Morse, Christopher, 109
mother tongue, 32–41
Mr. Ives' Christmas (Hijuelos), 120
mysterium tremendum, 27–32, 79

Nag Hammadi, 66, 76
narrative hermeneutics, 45–49
narrative hymns, 8–9
narrative preaching
    ambiguity of narrative and, 8
    characteristics of, xiii
    as congregational canon, 20–21
    critics of, 1–2, 7–18
    as dress rehearsal, 18–20
    history of, 6–7
    as means for remembering the lost
        and silenced, 21–22
    megachurch preachers and, 14–15
    Narrativity theses and, 10–11, 14
    as process for coming to faith, 22–25
    revisions for, 18–26
    rise of, 2–7
    value and uses of, 18–26
    See also preaching
Narrativity theses, 10–11, 14
National Geographic, 60
neo-gnosticism. *See* gnosticism
Neoplatonism, 95
new gnosticism. *See* gnosticism
New Testament. *See specific books of the
    Bible*
New York Times, 73
Nicaea, Council of, 59, 70
Nicene Creed, 92
Niebuhr, H. Richard, 19
Nietzsche, Friedrich, 41, 70
Noah, 51–53
Nock, Arthur Darby, 70, 77

No Country for Old Men (novel and
    film), 120–22

Old Testament. *See specific books
    of the Bible*
O'Regan, Cyril, 77, 81–83, 88,
    139n11
Origen, 68
orthodoxy, 70, 87–89, 138n27
Orwell, George, 87
Osteen, Joel, 120

Pagels, Elaine, 62, 63–65, 68–69,
    75–76, 81, 83
panentheism, 108
pantheism, 98–101
Pantocrator, 93
Patte, Daniel, 43–45
Paul
    on Areopagus, 108
    on the body, 96
    eschatology and, 119
    gnostic thought and, 68, 77
    on God, 99
    on Jesus Christ, 96
    missionary activities of, 61
    preaching and, 13, 35, 36, 43–45,
        53, 109
    on resurrection, 70
    shipwreck and, 21
    on sin, 72
    trial of, before King Festus, 61
Peace Like a River (Enger), 120
Pearson, Birger, 73, 90
Pentecostals, 79–80
persecution of Christians, 71–72
Philip, Gospel of, 56, 75–76
Poetics (Aristotle), 45
Poetics of Biblical Narrative, The (Alter),
    23–24
Poetics of Biblical Narrative, The
    (Sternberg), 23
Polkinghorne, John, 128–29
Possidius, 39
postmillennialism, 113–16. *See also*
    eschatology
prayer, 99, 127

preaching
Augustine and, 5–6, 18, 39–41
Barth on, 35
Calvin on, 20
current challenges to, xiii–xv
didactic approach to, 2–3
Emerson on, 6–7
eschatological preaching, 125–32
Eucharist compared with, 25
exegesis and, 42–45, 50–53
intellectual challenges presented in,
    63, 108–9
language of the gospel and, 34–41
loss of eschatology in, 112–17
loss of present tense in, 29–53
mimesis and, 46–50
mimetic exegesis and, 50–53
as multilingual activity, 32–33
multiple voices of, 18
narrative hermeneutics and, 45–49
to neo-gnostics, 106–10
Paul and, 13, 35, 36, 43–45, 53, 109
purpose of, 5–6, 18
See also narrative preaching
Preaching Jesus (Campbell), 9
Preaching Paul (Patte), 43–45
Preaching the Story, 4
prefiguration, 46, 49
Presbyterian Church, 112–13
present tense
Augustine on, 45
hiding from holy mystery and, 29–34
losing our mother tongue and, 32–41
loss of, in preaching, 29–53
mimetic exegesis and, 50–53
renewing vision and recovery voice,
    41–49
Ricoeur on, 45
Princeton University Chaplains' Advi-
    sory Council, 123–24
progress, 117–18
progressive Christianity, 87–88
The Protestant Hour radio program, 5
Proverbs, book of, 38
Psalms, 42
psychological Narrativity thesis, 10–11
Puritan theology, 116

Purpose-Driven Life, The (Warren), 120

Real Presences (Steiner), 41
refiguration, 49
religious pluralism, 101
repressed, return of, 117–25
"Requiem" (Akhmatova), 22
resurrection, 37–38, 70, 71, 73–74,
    108–10, 125
Revelation, book of, 11, 129–31
Reynolds, David, 6
Ricoeur, Paul, 22, 24, 45–50, 106
Road, The (McCarthy), 120
Robinson, James M., 138n27
Roman Catholic Church. See Catholic
    Church
Romans, Epistle to, 72, 124
Rutledge, Fleming, 15–18

Sacks, Oliver, 24–25
Saddleback Church, 119–20
saints, 22
salvation, 92–95, 119
Schweitzer, Albert, 106, 110
scientific rationalism, 30–33, 41
scriptures. See Bible; and specific books
    of the Bible
second coming of Christ, 112–13,
    114, 121
Secular Age, A (Taylor), 32
secularity, 30–32
Secundicus, 39
Senior, Donald, 60
Sense of an Ending, The (Kermode),
    127
sermons. See narrative preaching;
    preaching
Shawshank Redemption, The, 122–23
Sholl, Bryan K., 66–67
sin, 72, 87, 91–94, 110
Sleeth, Ron, 7–8
social justice. See justice
soul, 73–74, 112
Southern Baptists, 79–80
Soviet Union, 22
spirituality and spiritual quests, 61–64,
    67, 97, 101. See also gnosticism

Spong, John Shelby, 61–64, 74, 81, 83, 91
Springer, Jerry, 112
Steimle, Edmund, 5
Steiner, George, 41–42
Sternberg, Meir, 23
"Stories to Live By" (Wuthnow), 49
story preaching. See narrative preaching
Strawson, Galen, 10–12, 14, 46
Stringfellow, William, 131–32
Stroup, George, 36
subtraction story, 31–33
suffering, 15–17, 22, 72–73, 82, 86, 95–96, 99–100, 127
systematic theology, 120

Talmage, T. DeWitt, 6
Taylor, Barbara Brown, 5
Taylor, Charles, 31–33
Tertullian, 68
testimony, 22
Texas, 120
Text and Texture (Fishbane), 42–43
theodicy. See evil; suffering
theological left. See liberalism; and specific theologians
theological right. See conservatism; evangelicals; and specific theologians
Thomas, Gospel of, 56, 76
Thomas, Grace, 19–20

Thompson, James W., 8
Tillich, Paul, 98
Time and Narrative (Ricoeur), 45–49
Todd, John M., 27–28
transcendent, 30–31
Troeltsch, Ernst, 117
True North (Harrison), 75–76
Truth, Sojourner, 34–35
Turner, James, 118
Twain, Mark, 55
Twitchell, Rev. Joseph, xi-x
Tyrell, Georte, 105

Unitarianism, 6, 116
United Church of Christ, 112–13
USA Today, 60

Valentinian gnosticism, 139n11
Vermont, 36–37

Walsch, Neale Donald, 97–98
Warren, Rick, 119–20
Welker, Michael, 21
Wesley, John, 7
White, Andrew Dickson, 116
Wilberforce, Bishop Samuel, 118
Wilmore, Gayraud S., 123
wisdom, 37–38
Wright, N. T., 71–72
Wuthnow, Robert, 49